HISTORY

OF

THE WALDENSES,

FROM THE

EARLIEST PERIOD TO THE PRESENT TIME.

By
Paul Tice
and the author of The Lives of Wickliffe, Huss, Jerome, etc.

REVISED BY THE COMMITTEE OF PUBLICATION OF THE
AMERICAN SUNDAY SCHOOL UNION.

THE BOOK TREE
SAN DIEGO, CALIFORNIA

First published 1829
American Sunday School Union
Philadelphia, PA

ISBN 1-58509-099-9

Cover layout & design
Lee Berube

Printed on Acid-Free Paper
in the United States of America

Published by
The Book Tree
P O Box 16476
San Diego, CA 92176
www.thebooktree.com
We provide fascinating and educational products to help awaken the public to new ideas and
information that would not be available otherwise.
Call 1 (800) 700-8733 for our *FREE BOOK TREE CATALOG*.

INTRODUCTION

The story of the Waldenses is one of the greatest spiritual sagas the world has ever known, yet few people have heard of them. Their story deserves to be told because, in spite of the terrible persecution they have endured, their heritage is still alive and well today.

The Waldenses lived throughout Europe, but mostly in the northwestern part of Italy and across into France. Most of the serious problems were experienced in the 1500's, but it was not until 1848 when laws were finally passed officially giving the Waldenses religious freedom. Most of this book was first published in 1829, a time when holding such beliefs was still unlawful—so the author may have chosen to remain anonymous for the sake of his own protection. It is good he wrote the book, however, because the information he chose to share was relatively fresh, and not lost or forgotten as can sometimes happen.

Very little has been written from their point of view, in fact it was always claimed that everything we know about them was written by their opponents. Those making this claim had apparently never heard of this book.

The Waldenses were devout Christians who tried to follow the original teachings of Jesus to the best of their abilities. They followed what the Bible taught and nothing else, yet were up against a church that had changed in that respect. In their opinion certain forms of corruption had surfaced in the Church that they wished to have nothing to do with.

This book tells of their struggle to survive against a larger and more powerful opponent. Their faith, however, caused them to stand up for their beliefs no matter what the odds were against them. This book provides a powerful testimony for a people whose story has, in large part, remained untold.

Not long ago I included a chapter on the Waldenses in a book I wrote called *Triumph of the Human Spirit: The Greatest Achievements of the Human Soul and How Its Power can Change Your Life*. That chapter is being reproduced here in order to combine this scarce but important material into one volume. My research into the subject involved extremely rare books and documents that took years to uncover—so had thought that I had successfully gathered together most of the information available on them. In finding this additional information, I was (happily) proven wrong. The older part of this book adds much more information to what I have contributed to it. Minor points sometimes don't agree but for the most part, the information meshes together well. I give a general historical overview first, in Part One—covering the high points of Waldensian history and sharing some powerful stories.

The remainder of the book fills in many gaps to what I share in the opening pages, plus adds additional details that would have otherwise been lost to history. Traditional Christians scoff at groups like the Waldenses, having been told by history that they were nothing but heretics and should be paid no notice. Yet the Waldenses attempted to be—and actually were—more Christian than those who claimed to be at the time. It is time for history to speak again—this time with a voice on the Waldenses' behalf, rather than those of their persecutors. For the sake of historical accuracy and the passion of those who fought for truth, I am immensely proud to be presenting and sharing this material.

Paul Tice

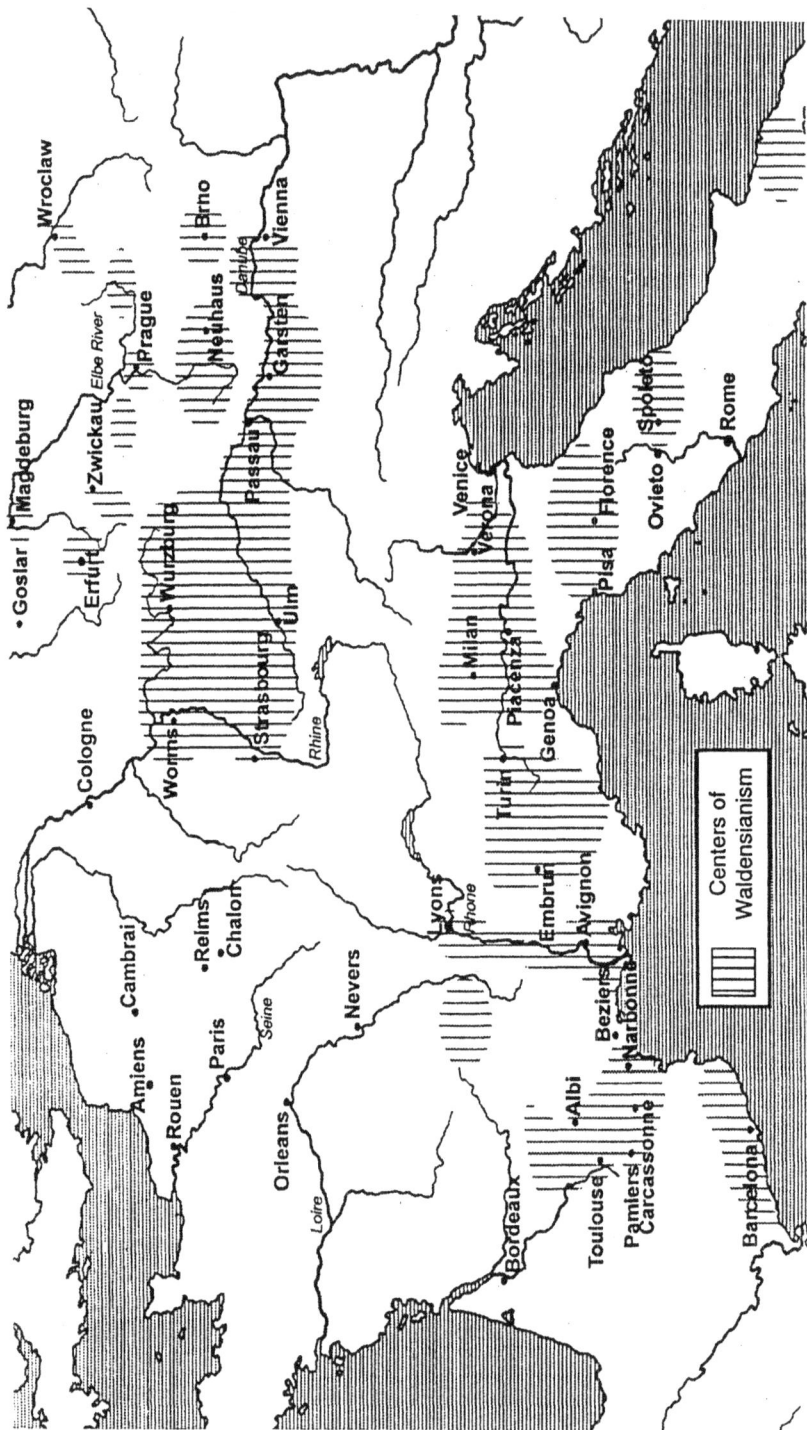

Waldensian Areas, 13th–15th centuries

Centers of Waldensianism

Goslar • Magdeburg • Wroclaw
Erfurt • Zwickau • Elbe River • Prague • Neuhaus • Brno
Cologne • Würzburg • Passau • Gastein • Vienna
Worms • Strasbourg • Ulm • Danube
Rhine
Amiens • Cambrai • Reims • Chalon
Rouen • Paris • Nevers • Seine
Orleans • Loire
Lyons • Rhône • Venice • Verona
Milan • Piacenza • Florence
Turin • Genoa • Pisa • Spoleto
Embrun • Avignon • Ovieto • Rome
Bordeaux • Albi • Béziers • Narbonne
Toulouse • Pamiers • Carcassonne
Barcelona

HISTORY OF THE WALDENSES
From the Earliest Period to the Present Time

Supplementary Text
by Paul Tice

The Waldenses

The knowledge we've retained on the Waldenses has been largely written by their opponents, all from a hostile point of view. Only through centuries of careful research have we been able to arrive at a more fair and complete picture of who these people were.

After the Dark Ages had ended by the eleventh century there began an awakening. It was a strange, spiritual awakening, recorded by historians of the time, which compelled thousands of humble people to undertake a pilgrimage of sorts from various towns and villages in the Balkans to the religious capital, Byzantium. These people tramped off in vast hordes under the guidance of people like Peter the Hermit and Walter the Penniless. No one could quite explain this phenomenon; it was a new thing to the historians who reported it. It suddenly seemed that people were truly "coming out of the dark." As these large numbers of common people sincerely searched for answers, three main resultant effects sprang forth, and took shape as separate movements.

First, there was a more pronounced support of the authority of the Gospels. Second, there developed an appeal for a life of renunciation and voluntary poverty, which soon turned into a rejection of the wealth and power of the Church. Third, there was a gradual spread of the Gnostic and Manichaean ideas relating to the origin of evil (Gnostic dualism). We are concerned here with the last two currents of thought.

Peter Waldo

The most enduring form of Gnostic dualism and the rejection of wealth was the Waldenses—a remnant survives even to this day in northern Italy. It was started by Peter Waldo, a wealthy resident of Lyons, France, who was not a priest or monk but a layman with a spiritual mission. The Bible was only available in Latin, and sometimes Greek. He started this entire movement because like most Frenchmen he was unable to read Greek or Latin, but wanted to study the Bible. He enlisted two clerics to translate various parts of the Bible, including the four Gospels, into the native Provencal language. He then read and reread the Bible many times. After doing so he realized his life had been running counter to Biblical teachings. One major concern was that he had been loaning money out at interest—something the Bible considered as usury, and believed his wealth had been gained at the expense of his soul.

This realization had hit Waldo like a ton of bricks, and is one of the most important (and most common) among people who are led by the spirit. Great things can be accomplished when one follows the heart instead of the pursuit of money. Waldo went on to do exactly that.

Around the year 1176, wealthy as he was, Waldo announced that he was giving all of his possessions to the poor and would become a traveling preacher. He owned a vineyard, a mill and a bakery, as well as estates of fields, forests and meadows. The more common and romantic story is that he indeed gave his belongings to the poor, but it seems there was, in reality, a problem. His wife stepped in and complained to the archbishop of Lyons, who then forbade Waldo to preach without authorization. Waldo ignored this gag order.

The real estate and other possessions, aside from his money, were turned over to his wife, whom he then abandoned. He left a generous dowry for his two unmarried daughters (one account claims he bought entry for them into a convent), gave all his remaining money to the poor, then set about preaching throughout the land, dressed in a simple robe, with various disciples in tow. His main message was that the obsession with money and power causes the death of the spirit, and that one should focus on living life simply, as the apostles had done.

His followers were all quite poor, so they were commonly called "The Poor Men of Lyons." All of the teachings were derived entirely from the Bible, and the Church had no problem with the movement—at first. The Waldenses goal was to live moral Christian lives. They did not reject the Church in any way, and Waldo either went to Rome in 1179 or sent a delegation there to ask the pope for recognition.

It is said that the Pope, Alexander III, first received Waldo as a favorite son and embraced his work and ideas. But he hesitated to approve him. After dwelling a bit, the pope sanctioned the Waldensian vows of poverty and gave permission for them to preach, subject to the approval of the archbishop. The archbishop declined the approval. Why? The Waldenses held no doctrines at variance with Church teachings at this time. The issue was that the Waldenses had translated the Bible into the native Provencal language, and had presented to the pope a book containing certain Biblical sections, translated, and additional commentaries on the Psalms. This gave people a direct understanding instead of relying on Church interpretations. The Waldenses felt they could draw insight directly from their Bibles as opposed to the Roman Church.

The Church decided it did not want this type of support, so told Waldo and his followers that they were not allowed to preach under any circumstances unless the clergy specifically asked them. And they weren't asking. Knowledge is power, and the people were to have none.

Waldo first abided by this ruling, but his conscience began to bother him. He was shocked at this opposition, and felt he had a calling. He was not a priest, but neither did he see himself as a Church antagonist. He and the Church were both trying to save souls and all that he was doing was intended to help, not compete with, the Church. Waldo's "sin" was that he had not been appointed by the Church in the first place, to do his work.

In Acts 5 Peter says:

We must obey God rather than men.

Peter Waldo gave this Bible passage much thought, and then continued his preaching. His followers spread from southern France, into Italy, and countries beyond.

The Bible as Authority

The Waldenses believed in the complete obedience to the commands of the Gospels, which they followed. The Bible to them was supreme, and anything it did not authorize had no place with them. Their criticism of Church doctrine clearly developed after their rejection by the Church. With only the Bible as their guide, they found, upon close study, that the Church deviated from Biblical principles in a number of areas. This is why they denounced additional doctrines like indulgences, holy water, excommunications, images, church music, worship of the cross, prayers in Latin (since no one could understand it), the adoration of saints, and various other statutes of the Church. These things were totally unnecessary to the Waldenses and not supported by the Bible.

They believed marriage to be open to all, including priests, since it is not forbidden in the New Testament. The existence of the priesthood itself was questioned since no trace of it exists in the Bible.

Although there were Waldensian churches, some Waldensians did not believe that worshipping in a church was necessary, calling them "heaps of stone." They based this on Acts 18:24 which states, "God... does not live in shrines made by men."

Their major criticism of Church doctrine was directed against the idea of purgatory. Purgatory presumably gives people the chance to purify themselves after death instead of going to either heaven or to hell. The Waldensians found that absolutely nothing is said in the Bible about this intermediary state, and that the idea originated in the sixth century. Salvation is not earned after death, it is only earned while alive. They believed that the doctrine of Christ and his apostles was all that was required for salvation, without all of the other window dressings of the Church, as listed above. A majority of people, especially in southern France, agreed.

Another point of major importance was their refusal to acknowledge the authority of the pope. Peter Waldo was the first person to accuse the pope of being the antichrist. He wondered, then asked, What Biblical authority did the pope have when he indirectly attacked a group, the Waldensians, who were following the Bible explicitly?

Back during the time of Emperor Constantine, there was supposedly a document put forth by him called the Donation of Constantine. This document seemingly transferred all earthly power from the Emperor to the papacy (Pope Sylvester I). The Waldensians considered this an act of seduction. They termed the Vatican a house of lies and the pope was the "Head of Error." Papal authority used this document as their basis for worldly authority until 1440, when Lorenzo Valla proved it, beyond a doubt, to be a forgery. *The papacy was never put in charge of the Church by Constantine.* To this day, the papacy has no rightful authority (other scriptural "proofs" hold little water), and the Waldensians were the first people to point this out.

In 1182 Waldo and his followers were driven out of Lyons by the Catholic authorities. This did little good, however, since by this time the movement had spread into northern Italy—and was continuing to spread throughout France.

The Church Lashes Back

In 1184 a Papal constitution was issued by Pope Lucius III denouncing the Waldenses and they were excommunicated as an entire group. At the same time, they were welcomed in Milan, Italy, and were allowed to build a church.

By 1208 Pope Innocent III, in a desperate attempt to replace this popular movement, created his own "Poor Catholics" using a former Waldensian to run it. This Catholic outfit was identical to the Waldenses except for being controlled entirely by the Church and practiced only the beliefs stamped with the Church's approval. But the Church was abundantly wealthy! Creating a group of "Poor Catholics" was a sham. The Waldensian's were opposed to the high life, excesses, and corruption of the Church which was being financed more and more by common (and poor) folk who had worked hard for the money which was ultimately used by the Church.

The Waldensians are often considered to be the first reformers, or at least they were attempting to do so, predating Luther and, to some degree, setting the stage for him. Indulgences and other corruption was rampant and staunchly opposed by them. The idea of buying salvation for the human soul angered and sickened them, as well as the un-Christian lifestyle of the higher ranking clergy.

By 1205, the year that Peter Waldo died, the Waldensian movement had been weakened. Waldo had no idea that his movement would gain strength and survive for more than 800 additional years. The weakness resulted from the Waldenses being split into two separate factions—the French Waldensians, known as The Poor Men of Lyons, who rejected marriage, manual labor, and a sedentary lifestyle; and the North Italian branch, the Poor Lombards, who accepted these practices and were thrown out of the Waldensian movement by Waldo himself, shortly before his death. Unlike the French, the Italian Lombards believed that marrying, having children, working hard, and being mobile would strengthen their communities and insure their survival.

After Waldo's death, events occurred which brought these two factions together. As early as 1212 (in Strasberg), Waldensians were burned at the stake. The extermination of the entire sect was demanded in 1215 by the great Catholic council known as the Fourth Lateran. As a result, thousands of Waldensians retreated to the foothills and remote valleys of the Western Alps. They called a secret meeting in 1218 and the French Waldensians adopted the more practical attitudes of the Italians—and began living in ways which would support their growth. They were facing a common enemy and if history had taught them anything, it was that they had to pull together if they were going to survive.

They made a wise decision. In 1233 the Inquisition was officially unleashed on the Waldenses, and the assault continued for centuries. They would not and could not be broken. The Waldenses were fighting against the clear corruption and materialistic greed of the Church and would never back down. Others who opposed the Church, even if they were not Waldensians, sought refuge in the Alpine wilderness and were welcomed warmly. In return, the Church hunted Waldensians as a group and individually. Messages sent between Waldensian communities were often coded to prevent an understanding by the prying eyes of the Inquisitors.

Their spiritual teachings also seem encoded within the mysterious symbolism of today's tarot cards. For instance, the Death card shows a skeleton on horseback, stampeding over the pope, the king, two cardinals, and a bishop. At the time, only the Waldensians knew the true meanings of the cards. Gypsies were the first to use them regularly, and carried them near and far. Since then, tarot cards have evolved into our modern playing cards. The belief that playing cards are a "tool of the devil," in addition to the tarot, has persisted in some circles to this day—mainly because of their Waldensian origin,

In 1320 a Waldensian was condemned to be burned by the future Pope Benedict XII (then Bishop) in Pamiers. The townspeople protested, saying this was a great holy man. They said the Bishop himself was the one to be burned because of the unfair tax burdens and other payments he required. It's unclear whether the man was saved or not, but it is clear that the townspeople had their priorities in proper order.

In a move likely aimed to combat the Waldenses, Pope John XXII declared, in 1323, that the idea of Jesus and the apostles living in voluntary poverty was heretical. Regardless of the real truth—that Jesus had actually done so—the Church had plenty of money at this time and wasn't about to start promoting voluntary poverty.

In the year 1380 two Inquisitors named Martin of Prague and Peter Zwicker were commissioned to arrest and try to convert all Waldenses throughout Europe. By the end of the fourteenth century the Church had so many Waldenses locked in jail, there was not enough food to feed them. Pope Gregory IX appealed for donations and food for the prisoners but it wasn't enough. In

Grenoble 150 of them were burned in just one day in 1393. At about the same time, Waldenses in Austria were burning down many of the clergy's homes that served as bases for Inquisitors. This was one of the few times Waldenses had become violent, but by this time it was clear that the Inquisitors wanted the Waldenses dead—all of them.

When the Hussite revolution was taking place in the early 1400's, word of it reached the Waldenses. They immediately sent several "barbas," or teachers, to Bohemia to witness first-hand what was happening. What followed was a series of meetings between leaders of both groups that helped the Waldensians immensely. The barbas received theological training from the Hussites and, as a result, began to read theological works in Latin, use higher level mathematics, and practice medicine enough to deal with minor diseases. Young Waldensians were taken on in apprentice programs, and the strength of their movement grew because of help from the Hussites.

A century later, when the Reformation broke out, Waldenses lent their support to the Protestants. At this point, the Waldenses had been in existence for almost 350 years, and were ready to help others with similar ideas.

European "Witchcraft"

Witches had been hunted in scattered parts of Europe since the mid 1200's, but it was the Church's reaction to the Waldenses that gave focus to their persecutions. This process began around 1380, when heretics in the Alps were forced under torture to confess to having celebrated a nocturnal orgy. Those present were allegedly forced to drink a disgusting liquid made from the excrement of a giant toad that one of the Waldensians kept under her bed. Those who consumed the drink fell under the spell of the sect and were unable to leave it. Such stories spread and by 1399 a book was written called *Errors of the Waldensian Heresy*, which accused them of ritual sex, child sacrifice, and the worship of Lucifer—the same accusations given later to witches. By about 1430 the word "Waldensian" had become synonymous with the word "witch." At this same time, women were first depicted in books as flying through the air on broomsticks. They were Waldensian women.

In France in 1404, before the major witch craze had blossomed, two men named Anthony Fabri and Christopher de Salience were commissioned to persecute the Waldenses of Dauphiny. They killed many and confiscated the property and goods of others. When Louis XII became king in 1498 the Waldenses, now considered "witches," approached him and asked restitution of their property from the Church. He sided with the Waldenses and made every effort to restore their property, but got stonewalled by the Church at every turn and was unable to succeed. Nevertheless, the King of France sided with this group of so-called heretics, recognizing their rights to property at a time when they were being terribly persecuted.

These persecutions had increased in the year 1484, when Pope Innocent VIII took the papal throne. He was immediately approached by two Dominican Inquisitors, Heinrich Kramer and James Sprenger (authors of the *Malleus Maleficarum*), who complained that they were being impeded by local ecclesiastical authorities in their zealous persecutions of witches. What resulted was the Bull of 1484, giving them full authority to carry out their terrible deeds. But the main reason for the edict was to officially transfer the crimes of witchcraft to the Waldenses. They were accused within the bull of engaging in sorcery, so as to arouse the people against them by mixing and confusing their beliefs with sorcery. People would now be afraid to become or continue to be Waldensian because they could then be arrested and/or killed as a witch. And the public at large would begin to see them all in this inaccurate light more clearly. This terrible, unethical act of deception was very harmful to the honest people engaged in the Waldensian faith and it declined sharply thereafter.

A Popular Faith

Although the Church treated the Waldenses as enemies, Peter Waldo had never intended to start a separate church. He was attempting to act as a "free agent" for and within the Church. It seems his only crime was believing that his mission came from God, and not the clergy. In many parts of France during the 13th and 14th centuries the Waldensian faith became the official religion, sharing the honors with the more notorious Cathars, who claimed the remaining areas. In the 1200's there was a Waldensian named De Vaux and a Cathar named William of Ayros who went from village to village and home to home, spending as much time healing the sick as they did preaching sermons. These two movements grew closer together because of the persecution they were both receiving from the Church.

One difference between the Waldenses and Cathars was that the Waldenses believed in the humanity and physical suffering of Christ, whereby the Cathars believed Christ did not suffer physically on the cross because he was supernatural to a degree.

With both movements taking over the land, Catholic churches were abandoned and ones that didn't fall into ruins were used primarily by the Waldenses for services.

The Roman Church was stunned. Their highest-ranking clergy were related to the noble families of the region who themselves favored the Cathars—so early in this movement they were powerless. They desperately hurried and became more organized. The Inquisition became more focused over time and many Waldensians were systematically killed or jailed. Although specifically targeted, they managed to survive in Italy into the 15th century and beyond. Switzerland also provided them safety for a time. In 1488 they retreated into the Alpine Valley of Italy after a Crusade was organized against them (1487-89), but it failed because of the inaccessible mountains. In later years, other crusades would follow.

Persecution Intensifies

By the early 1500s only small pockets of Waldenses remained in Europe. One place they were thriving was in the Piedmont valleys of France, across from Italy, where they had been mostly left alone. The last holdouts in France were closely connected to those across the border in Italy and were quite likely part of the same group (the geographic area they inhabited covered both countries). They had enjoyed relative freedom here but Pope Paul III was a passionate bigot, so upon taking the papal throne in 1533 he solicited the Parliament in Turin to persecute the Waldenses. The Protestant movement had just begun, and the Church saw a dangerous alliance forming between Protestants and Waldenses. Therefore, the Parliament agreed to persecute and a number of Waldenses were immediately captured and burned at the stake.

It was soon decided that deputies would be sent into the valleys of Piedmont carrying the following propositions:

1) That if the Waldenses would return into the fold of the Roman Catholic Church, they would be allowed to live on their land, with their families, and within their homes without any molestation.

2) That to prove their obedience, they should send 12 of their foremost representatives, along with all their schoolmasters and ministers, to Turin, to be "dealt with at discretion."

3) That the Duke of Savoy, the King of France, and the Pope all approved of and authorized the proceedings of the Parliament of Turin upon this occasion.

4) That if the Waldenses of Piedmont rejected these propositions, persecution and death would be their reward.

The Waldenses received these four articles and answered them with four equal replies which stated:

1) That no consideration whatsoever would make them renounce their religion.

2) That they would never consent to entrusting their most loved and respected friends to the custody and discretion of their worst enemies.

3) That they valued the approbation of the King of kings, who reigns in heaven, far more than any temporal authority.

4) That their souls were more precious than their bodies.

This infuriated the pope and Parliament. The Waldenses, like the Protestants, recognized scripture as the only source of religious truth. They refused to bow down to an organization that went contrary to what scripture states. The Alpine Waldenses proceeded to make friendly contact and compared notes with the most zealous Protestants of the time—the Swiss Calvinists—and through this contact became recognized as a Protestant sect.

The Church was able to catch only a few more stray heretics to burn, then decided to solicit an army from the king to exterminate them all. As the troops were about to march, news came that the Protestant princes of Germany were prepared to send their own troops in defense of the Waldenses. There was a strong connection at the time between the Waldenses, the Protestants, and the Hussites from that region (followers of John Hus). The recent Protestant success had created a powerful brotherhood. The King of France did not want an all out war, so recalled his soldiers and informed Parliament that he could not spare any troops at the time.

A few years later, a representative of the pope visited the Duke of Savoy on business and told the prince that he was surprised he had not either exterminated the Waldenses from the

Piedmont valleys or convinced them to return to the Church. This conduct, the Duke was informed, had aroused this representative's suspicion into thinking the Duke was possibly a heretic or at least favored them, and that he would have to report this to the pope. The Duke resolved to prove his faith by going after the Waldenses with a vengeance.

He ordered all Waldenses to attend Catholic mass regularly, under penalty of death. When they refused, he entered the valleys with troops and began a furious persecution. In April of 1545 three thousand unarmed Waldensians were slaughtered. Some were caught and served life sentences as galley slaves on French ships. Those who escaped fled with what little belongings they could carry. Homes were plundered, then burnt to the ground—22 villages in all. If a schoolmaster or minister was caught, he was tortured terribly. Small children were taken from their families and put with Roman Catholic nurses to be raised. In one incident, twenty-five terrified women who sought shelter in a cave were suffocated by a fire that was built at its mouth.

For the Duke of Savoy, these victories were not enough. He required more troops because his success was not complete, so commanded a general release of all jailed criminals provided that, once free, they would agree to battle the Waldenses. When news of this reached the Waldenses, they gathered their possessions and retreated higher into the Alps, among the rocks and caves, some as far as Switzerland. Although the army was able to burn abandoned towns and villages, they could not get to the people themselves, who defended the narrow passes from safe cover and repulsed their enemies. The Protestant powers of Germany did, at this time, join forces and helped them in their cause. (In crucial moments throughout history, Germany was always ready to help the Waldenses.) Because of this, the Waldenses were able to return from the mountains and back into villages before the harsh winter set in.

A Change of Heart

The Duke of Savoy was frustrated since the Waldenses were now back in their towns, rebuilding or staying with friends. It had cost the Duke much money, and he had expected the resulting plunder to repay him for his efforts and expenses. It didn't. Most of the wealth was taken by the pope's assistant and various monks and bishops who attended the Duke's army, using a variety of ruses and excuses to get paid. The Duke decided to make peace with the Waldenses. It wasn't worth it, fighting them at your own expense and getting double-crossed by the papacy. Before the peace treaty was signed, the Duke died—but he instructed his son and heir to be as favorable as possible to the Waldenses. He did as his father requested and ratified the peace agreement, although the priests and bishops did all they could to prevent it.

A Spiritual Triumph

This legacy of peace continues to the present day—evidenced by the Waldenses themselves, who continue to live in this area. In their early years, these people paid dearly for their chosen beliefs, unlike today when the price is far less. Their trials were enormous, but they survived. A law passed in 1848 gave religious freedom to all Waldensians.

The Waldensian Church has also survived. Today it is a member of the Federal Council of Protestants, and the Reformed and Presbyterian Alliance. Churches exist in Italy (about 120), southern France, Switzerland, Argentina, Uruguay, and have in recent years been known to exist in the United States in Texas, North Carolina, and Missouri. In Italy, at least 50,000 Waldensians live and worship freely. The largest Protestant church in Italy is operated by Waldensians. It is located in Rome.

Despite almost 400 brutal years of persecution, their spirit and faith lives on. During the worst years of bloody persecutions against them, they consoled themselves with what had become their motto: "The light shines in the darkness." This may be a paraphrase from John 1:5, which reads,

The light shines on in the dark,
and the darkness has never mastered it.

If someone is more powerful than you are, physically, it doesn't necessarily mean that they are spiritually superior. The Waldenses proved this by using the power of the spirit and they survived against all odds. Their presence today earmarks their incredible triumph.

HISTORY

OF

THE WALDENSES.

——»»❀❀❀««——

CHAPTER I.

In the darkest ages of Popery, God never
"left himself without a witness."   It is true,
that from the rise of that Antichristian power
till the dawn of the Reformation, the people
of Christ may be emphatically denominated a
"little flock;" yet small as their number may
appear to have been to the eye of man, and
unable as historians may now be to trace with
accuracy the saints of the Most High, amidst
"a world lying in wickedness," it cannot be
doubted that, even then, there was "a remnant which kept the commandments of God,
and the testimony of Jesus Christ."   If God
reserved to himself "seven thousand in Israel
who had not bowed the knee to Baal," in the
reign of the idolatrous Ahab, can we suppose,
that, during any succeeding period, his Church
has ceased to exist, or that his cause has utterly perished?

Among others who fearlessly lifted up their voices against the evils which abounded in the Church, was a body of Christians, called Paulicians, (from the Apostle Paul,) who appeared in the east about the year 660. Constantine, their leader, who was a native of an obscure town in the vicinity of Samosata, having received from a stranger the New Testament in its original language, not only studied that inestimable gift himself, but communicated to others the great truths which it contained. The success which attended his labours was so great, that a church was soon collected, and in a short time afterwards several individuals arose among them qualified for the work of the ministry. These heralds of the gospel disseminated their principles in many distant places; several congregations were formed throughout Armenia and Cappadocia, and in process of time they spread over the provinces of Asia Minor to the westward of the Euphrates.

Alarmed at the growing importance and rapid increase of this new sect, the Greek Emperors persecuted them with the most cruel severity. Their books were committed to the flames, and their persons subjected to capital punishments. Constantine, their leader, was the first victim to the cruelty of their enemies, having been stoned to death by order of a Greek officer. Multitudes of his followers soon shared a like fate; and during a period of one hundred and fifty years, these unoffending people were subjected to the most horrid persecutions; all which they endured with Christian meekness and patience. " The more they were oppressed," however, " the more they multiplied and grew." The persecution had, however, some intermission, until at length Theodora, the Greek Empress, exerted herself against them beyond all her predecessors. She sent inquisitors throughout all Asia Minor in search of the Paulicians, and is computed to have killed, by the gibbet, by fire, and by the sword, *a hundred thousand persons.*

Though it would appear that the faith and patience of the Paulicians at length failed, and that towards the close of the ninth century they were gradually betrayed into a secular spirit, yet many others were raised up by Divine Providence, who firmly and nobly withstood the Papal usurpations. Among these, none were more eminent than Paulinas, Bishop of Aquileia, in Italy, and Claudius, Bishop of Turin. In regard to Claudius of Turin, it will be necessary to enter a little into detail, not only from the title which he has commonly received from ecclesiastical historians, namely, that of the " first Protestant Reformer," but more particularly on account of his being considered by some as the proper founder of the WALDENSES.* This eminent saint was a native of Spain, and in his early years was one of the chaplains in the court of Lewis the Meek, King of France. That monarch, perceiving the ignorance of a great part of Italy, was desirous of providing the churches of Piedmont with a person who would oppose the growing idolatry of image-worship, and seeing none better qualified for accomplishing this object than Claudius, on account of his extensive knowledge of the Scriptures, and eminentt alents as a preacher, Lewis raised him to the see of Turin, in 817. Claudius performed the duties of his office with great faithfulness; and, both by writing and preaching, incessantly laboured to instruct the people in the great truths of the gospel of Christ. Many of the doctrines which were taught by this Reformer, were directly the reverse of those which were received and inculcated by the Romish Church, and coincided with those which were afterwards adhered to by the Waldenses. He affirmed that the only proper head of the Church is the Lord Jesus Christ,—a doctrine which struck at the very root of the Popish hierarchy.

The attacks of Claudius on the kingdom of darkness, were highly resented by the ad-

* The words Waldenses, Vallenses, and Vaudois, have the same meaning, viz. *inhabitants of the valley.*

nerents of Popery. The monks reviled him as a blasphemer and a heretic, and his own people became so refractory, that in a short time he went about in fear of his life.—Claudius says of himself, " Being obliged to accept the bishopric, when I came to Turin, I found all the churches full of abominations and images; and because I began to destroy what every one adored, every one began to open his mouth against me. They say, we do not believe that there is any thing divine in the image; we only reverence it in honour of the person whom it represents. I answer, if they who have quitted the worship of devils, honour the images of the saints, they have not forsaken idols; they have only changed the names. For whether you paint upon a wall the pictures of Peter or Paul, or those of Jupiter, Saturn, or Mercury, they are now neither gods, nor apostles, nor men; the name is changed, but the error remains the same. If men must be adored, there would be less absurdity in adoring them when alive, while they are the image of God, than after they are dead, when they only resemble stocks and stones."

Such were the sentiments of Claudius regarding the worship of images, and such his devotion to that pure worship which alone is well pleasing to Jehovah. Nor were his labours in vain. By his preaching, and by his

writings, he disseminated the pure doctrines
of the gospel of Christ, as he found them contained in the Scriptures of truth; and he was
made the happy instrument of sowing that
seed, which being watered and blessed by the
influence of heaven, filled at length the valleys of Piedmont. These " valleys," says,
Jones, " were in time filled with his disciples,
and while midnight darkness sat enthroned
over almost every portion of the globe, the
Waldenses, which is only another name for
the inhabitants of these valleys, preserved
the gospel among them in its native purity
and rejoiced in its glorious light."

Notwithstanding the powerful opposition
which he experienced from the slaves of superstition, Claudius was suffered to end his
days in peace. From the persecuting spirit
of Popery, we cannot but conclude, that Claudius would have fallen a victim to the malice
of his enemies, had they not been afraid of
the French court, by whom he was protected.
His life, however, was in continual jeopardy.
" In standing up," says he, " for the defence
of the truth, I am become a reproach to my
neighbours, to that degree, that those who
see us do not only scoff at us, but point at us
one to another. But God, the father of
mercies, and author of all consolation, hath
comforted us in all our afflictions, that we
may be able, in like manner, to comfort

those that are cast down with sorrow and affliction."

Having spent an active and a useful life in the service of the Redeemer, and in promoting his cause in the world, this great Reformer died in peace, in the year 839.

CHAPTER II.

PREVIOUS to entering on the history of the Waldenses, it may be proper to give here a short description of the valleys which these faithful witnesses for the truth inhabited, and which were the scene of their long and dreadful sufferings. These valleys are for the most part situated within the confines of Piedmont,* and extend along the eastern foot of the Cottian Alps, the highest range of mountains in Europe, and which divide Italy from France, Switzerland, and Germany. The inhabitants were in former times the subjects of the dukes of Piedmont and Savoy, but more recently they have become subject to the king of Sardinia; and though they reside in a country which lies between France and

* This name, which signifies " at the foot of the mountains," is derived from Piedmont's being situated at the bottom of the Alps.

Italy, they do not entirely agree with either
nation in manners, customs, or language.

The principal valleys are, Aosta and Susa
on the north, Stura on the south, and in the
interior of the country, Lucerna, Angrogna,
Roccipiatta, Pramol, Perosa, and San Martino. The valley of Pragela, being surrounded
by very high mountains, in the sides of which
are numerous caves, formed one of the chief
places of retreat for the inhabitants in times
of persecution.* Angrogna, Pramol, and San

* The following description of one of the caverns into
which the Waldenses fled for safety from their persecutors, may give the reader some idea of the ingenuity
which these afflicted people were compelled to exert for
their own safety, as well as the natural asylums in many
of the mountains, which were afforded them by Divine
Providence. "Near the lofty and projecting crag which
soars above Mount Vaudelin, there was a natural cavern,
which the inhabitants of the commune of La Torre contrived to make a secret hiding place. This cavern, in
which between three and four hundred persons might
conceal themselves, was vaulted, and shaped not unlike
an oven, with clefts in the rock, which served for win-
dows, and even for loopholes; and prepared with recesses,
which answered the purpose of watch-houses, from
whence they might observe the motions of their assailants.
There were also several chambers within this vast cave,
accommodations for cooking meat, and a large fountain
well supplied with water. It was impossible to enter it,
except by one hole at the top; and those who were in the
secret, could only let themselves down one at a time, and
by a very slow and gradual process, with the assistance
of steps, or foot-holes, cut in the rock. In fact, it was
like descending into a mine; and one or two resolute men
might easily defend the entrance against the assault of
any force that could be brought against them."

Martino, are likewise strongly fortified by bulwarks of rocks and mountains; " as if the all-wise Creator," says Morland, " had from the beginning designed that place as a cabinet wherein to put some inestimable jewel; or, to speak more plainly, there to reserve many thousands of souls, which should not bow the knee before Baal."

Geographers and travellers in general, have described several of these valleys as being remarkably fertile, abounding in every thing necessary to the enjoyment of human life. The valley of Angrogna in particular, is thus described by Gilly: " Angrogna lies to the north of La Torre, and in the midst of some of the finest mountain scenery of which the Alps can boast. The mountain stream, which is called the torrent of Angrogna, gives its name to a cluster of valleys which branch out like the boughs of a tree, and runs into the Pelice, just below La Torre. It is supplied by innumerable springs of water, which gush from the rocks, and by following its course from the vale, the tourist will be conducted to the village itself; and higher up, to such a succession of picturesque spots, and secluded glens, as no description can do justice to. The natural beauties of the scenery of Angrogna, and the sublime objects of crag rising above crag, of enormous masses of rock retiring into the glens beneath, and of abysses, the depths of which the eye cannot penetrate, are rendered still more interesting by their being consecrated to the memory of heroes and martyrs, whose histories are in the mouth of every peasant.—Before we left the scenery of Angrogna, and took a last view of its match less beauties, we looked down upon a vale, the sweetest I ever saw, and which to this moment, after having seen the most lovely spots in Switzerland and Italy, I remember rather as a delightful vision, than a real prospect.　It lay in the midst of a circular chain of mountains, so sheltered and protected, that it looked as if no rough winds could ever visit it.　The declivities which sloped down to it were clothed with trees of every description, among which were abundance of walnuts, mulberries, chesnuts, cherry, and other fruit trees.

Though none of the other valleys are equally delightful, yet they are generally far from being unfruitful. But while the traveller may admire the beauty or the fertility of many of the valleys of Piedmont, the Christian will contemplate their far higher glory, in their having had early planted among them, what may justly be denominated " the vineyard of the Lord of Hosts," and the " trees of righteousness of his own hand planting." For here " thousands of the disciples of Christ, as will hereafter be shown, were found, even in the very worst of times, preserving the faith in its purity, adhering to the simplicity of Christian worship, patiently bearing the cross after Christ; men distinguished by their fear of God, and obedience to his will, and persecuted only for righteousness' sake."

Although we have stated in the former chapter, that Claudius of Turin has been styled the founder of the Waldensian Churches, their origin is to be traced to a period still more remote. Leger begins his history of the Churches of the Vaudois, by a declaration that " they never required any reformation." For the first four or five centuries, the whole of what is termed the diocess of the north of Italy, of which the Waldenses formed a part, remained comparatively pure. Though not altogether free from error and superstition in succeeding ages, yet being a pastoral, simple, and unambitious people, whose situation kept them at a distance from the controversies and customs of these degenerate ages, they remained comparatively little infected by the abounding evils in the Church. The most ancient Roman Catholic historian of the persecutions to which they were subjected, affirms, that " Toulouse had been scarcely ever exempt, even from its first foundation, from that pest of heresy which the fathers transmitted to their children;" and that " their opinions had been transmitted, in Gaul, from generation to generation, almost from the origin of Christianity." A noble testimony to the antiquity of these evangelical Churches, which, from the first planting of religion in Gaul, had, as far as their opportunities would allow, resisted the usurpations and corruptions of the Church of Rome. Pope Alexander III. in a synod held at Tours, in 1167, declared, "That the doctrine of the Vaudois was a damnable heresy of long continuance." And their adversary Reinier, an Italian inquisitor of the middle of the thirteenth century, whose business it was to report the opinions of the heretics of Lyons, gives the following singular testimony:—" The heresy of the Vaudois, or poor people of Lyons, is of great antiquity. Among all the sects that either are or have been, there is none more dangerous to the Church, and that for three reasons. I. Because it is the sect of the *longest standing of any;* for some say that it hath been continued down ever since the time of Pope Sylvester, (in the fourth century;) and others, ever since that of the Apostles. 2. Because it is the most general of all sects; for scarcely is there a country to be found where this sect hath not spread itself. And, 3. Because it has the greatest appearance of piety; for, in the sight of all, these men are just and honest in their transactions,—believe of God what ought to be believed,—receive all the articles of the Apostles' creed, and only profess to hate the Church of Rome."

The attention of the neighbouring Roman Catholic states was at length excited; and, finding that those Alpine valleys were filled with a people whose faith and practice were directly opposed to those of Rome, they left no means untried to overcome and compel them to submit to the yoke of spiritual despotism. Perceiving, however, that neither force nor fraud was sufficient to effect their purpose, they had recourse to the civil power, and demanded its aid in crushing heretics so contumacious. For some time the princes and nobility of the adjacent countries refused to interfere; but priestly authority and tyranny at length prevailed, and the inhabitants of Piedmont were subjected to all the horrors of persecution. Turin especially was the scene of numerous cruelties, and many eminent servants of the Redeemer there sealed their testimony with their blood. To avoid the storm of persecution, multitudes of the Piedmontese fled from their native valleys, and, crossing the Alps, sought refuge among the inhabitants of the surrounding countries. In Italy, Germany, France, and England, to which they retreated in the hope of finding an asylum, they not only succeeded in preserving the pure doctrines of their own secluded valleys, but, for a time, were the means of producing extraordinary effects upon the manners and character of the different people among whom they took up their abode.

Though these eminent witnesses for the truth are now termed generally WALDENSES and ALBIGENSES, yet they were formerly known by a variety of names,—some derived from their teachers, some from their manner of life, some from the places where they resided, some from the fate they suffered, and some from the malice of their enemies. The valleys of Piedmont, first gave them the name of Vallenses, Waldenses, or Vaudois, a name which has since been employed to distinguish them as a primitive church. Those in the south of France were termed Albigenses, or poor men of Lyons, from their residence in or about Albi and Lyons. In like manner, they were called Picards, Lombards, Bohemians, Bulgarians, &c. from the countries in which they dwelt. The epithets Cathari and Paterines, were applied to them as terms of reproach; and that of Lollards, either from the same cause, or from a Waldensian pastor, Walter Lollard, who flourished about the middle of the thirteenth century. They also received the names of Josephites, Arnoldists, Berengarians, &c. from some of their principal teachers: and, in order to render them odious in the eyes of the world, their enemies branded them with the names of several ancient heretics.

There were differences of opinion among these various classes of men, but of all of them it may be affirmed, that they ardently opposed the absurdities of the church, and the tyranny of the Papal see, and boldly preached, according to their light, "the truth as it is in Jesus." Whatever might be the errors, however, of any of these branches, the parent stock, the Waldenses of the valleys of Piedmont, never deviated from the pure doctrines of the word of God.

Having made these remarks concerning the various branches of opponents to the Romish church, who have all been denominated by the general term *Waldenses,* we shall now take notice more particularly of a number of sincere and humble Christians, who, in the beginning of the twelfth century, attracted the notice of the Papal see, and who, among other names, were by their enemies termed *Cathari.* They were found chiefly in the south of France, Savoy, and Milan; and in Cologne, Flanders, and Lombardy. Their doctrines resembled, in many particulars, those of Claudius of Turin; and it is not at all improbable that they were the fruit of his labours, and had existed from the age in which he lived. These heretics, as they were called by their enemies, were accused of holding the most detestable opinions; and many of them were put to death in the cruelest form, by the supporters of the Romish church.

One of their enemies, Evervinus, after throwing out innumerable invectives and false statements against a people, of whose manners he acknowledges he knew but little, with a strange inconsistency adds: "If you ask them of their faith, nothing can be more Christian; if you observe their conversation, nothing can be more blameless; and what they speak, they prove by deeds. You may see a man, for the testimony of his faith, frequent the church, honour the elders, offer his gift, make his confession, receive the sacrament. What more like a Christian? As to life and manners, he circumvents no man. He fasts much, and eats not the bread of idleness, but works with his hands for his support. The whole body, indeed, are rustic and illiterate, and all whom I have known of this sect are very ignorant."

Egbert, too, a monk, tells us, that he had often disputed with those heretics, and that *they maintained their sentiments by the authority of Scripture.* "They are armed," says he, "with all those passages in holy Scripture which in any degree seem to favour their sentiments; with these they know how to defend themselves, and to oppose the

Catholic faith; though they mistake entirely the true sense of Scripture, which cannot be discovered without great judgment. They are increased to great multitudes throughout all countries, to the great danger of the church; for their words eat like a canker. Concerning the souls of the dead, they hold this opinion, that at the very instant of their departure out of the body, they go to eternal bliss or endless misery, for they do not admit the belief of the Universal Church, that there are some purgatory punishments, with which the souls of some are tried for a time, on account of those sins from which they have not been purified by a plenary satisfaction in this life. On which account they think it superfluous and vain to give alms for the dead and to celebrate masses; and they scoff at our ringing of bells, which, nevertheless, for pious reasons, are used in our churches, to give others warning that they may pray for the dead. As for masses, they altogether despise them, regarding them as of no value."

During the twelfth century the Cathari were exposed to many grievous sufferings. Galdinus, archbishop of Milan, having for eight or nine years persecuted them with great barbarity, fell a martyr to his own zeal, in the year 1173, in consequence of an illness which he contracted through the excess of his vehemence in preaching against them.

A company of these poor despised people, consisting of about thirty men and women, appeared in England in 1159, and soon attracted the attention of the government by the singularity of their religious practices and opinions. They were immediately apprehended, and brought before a council of the clergy at Oxford. Being questioned concerning their religion, Gerrard their teacher, answered that they were Christians, and believed the doctrines of the Apostles. Upon a more particular inquiry, it appeared that they denied several of the received doctrines of the church, such as purgatory, prayers for the dead, the invocation of saints, &c.; and on refusing to abandon these *heretical* opinions, they were condemned as being incorrigible, and delivered over to the secular power to be punished. At the instigation of the clergy, the king, Henry II. commanded them to be branded with a red hot iron on the forehead, to be whipped through the streets of Oxford, and then, deprived of part of their clothes, to be turned out into the open fields, all persons being prohibited from affording them any shelter or relief, under the severest penalties. This cruel sentence was executed in its utmost rigour; and it being the depth of winter, they all perished with cold and hunger!

" Such was the provision of divine grace,"

says Milner, speaking of the true piety of the persecuted Waldenses, "to take out of a corrupt and idolatrous world of nominal christians, a people formed for himself, who should show forth his praise, and who should provoke the rest of mankind by the light of true humility and holiness; a people, singularly separate from their neighbours in spirit, manners, and discipline; rude indeed, and illiterate, and not only discountenanced, but even condemned, by the few real good men who adhered altogether to the Romish church; condemned because continually misrepresented. I know not a more striking proof of that great truth of the divine word, that, in the worst of times, the church shall exist, and the gates of hell shall not prevail against it."

CHAPTER III.

About the year 1160, Peter Waldo, a rich merchant of Lyons, attached himself to the Waldenses, at a period, happily, when the Papal hierarchy began to put its threats in execution against all who questioned its infallibility. The extensive mercantile engagements of this great and good man, gave ample opportunities of conversation with strangers on the idolatries of the Romish church; and his influence and riches enabled him with more boldness to take a decided part in opposing its usurped authority. Having clearly seen, from a careful perusal of the Scriptures, the only way of salvation through faith in the righteousness of Christ, he was exceedingly desirous of communicating the same knowledge of divine truth to others. For this purpose he abandoned his mercantile pursuits, distributed his wealth among the poor; and, while they flocked to him to partake of his alms, he laboured to impress upon their minds the paramount importance of eternal concerns. But the ardent desire of Waldo to instruct the ignorant, did not stop here. The Latin Bible was the only edition of the Scriptures at that time in Europe, and very few of the people being capable of reading it, this zealous reformer was led either to translate it himself, or procure it to be translated, into the vulgar tongue; thus having the honour of being the first who gave the word of God to the people in any modern language of Europe.* He also maintained, at his own expense, several persons who were employed

---

* It was not the whole of the sacred volume, however, but parts of it only, which were at this time translated into the French language. The first entire Bible in the French language was translated and printed by Robert Olivetan, a native of the valleys, at Neufchatel, about the year 1535.

to recite and expound his translation to the
people; and hence, most probably, proceeded
the opinion that he was the founder of the
Waldenses,—an opinion which the Roman
Catholics were glad to encourage; for it has
ever been their object to represent the Waldenses as a sect of recent date, and to vindi-
cate the antiquity of their own superstitions.

Being thus provided with copies of the
Scriptures in their own language, the opponents of the Romish church were encouraged
to declare themselves with greater boldness,
and enabled to prove that the doctrines of their
adversaries were in direct opposition to the
divine word. The consequences of all this
may be easily imagined. So soon as they
employed that invincible engine, the Scriptures in the vulgar tongue, they were immediately cursed and excommunicated. The
Archbishop of Lyons had already, in 1172,
peremptorily forbidden the new reformer "to
teach any more, on pain of excommunication,
and of being proceeded against as an heretic;"
and Waldo having replied, "that, though a
layman, he could not be silent in a matter
which concerned the salvation of his fellow
creatures," Pope Alexander III. cursed him
and his adherents, and commanded the Archbishop to proceed against him with the utmost
rigour. Waldo was therefore compelled to
leave Lyons; and so fierce was the rage of

the Romish adherents against him, that he
had to become a wanderer for the rest of his
life.   He took refuge at first in Dauphiny,
with an intention, probably, of finding his
way to the secluded valleys of Pragela or
Angrogna, among the Waldenses of Piedmont.   But finding that to be impossible,
from the rage of persecution in those places
through which he had to pass, he retired for
a short time to Picardy, where his labours
were attended with the most abundant success.   Being driven also from thence, he
proceeded to Germany, carrying with him
the glad tidings of salvation; and at length
he settled at Bohemia, where he died, after
having been engaged for nearly twenty years
in publicly instructing the people.   His doc
trines, spread extensively in many places;
and appear to have so harmonized with those
of the Waldenses in the valleys of Piedmont,
that, not without reason, they and his follow
ers were henceforward considered the same.

Enraged at the rapid spread of doctrines
which struck at the very root of Popery, the
supporters of that Antichristian system had
recourse to fire and sword, as the surest method of ridding themselves of adversaries so
dangerous.   Thirty-five citizens of Mentz
were burned in one fire in the city of Bingen,
and eighteen in Mentz.   The Bishops of
Mentz and Strasburgh were particularly ac-

tive in endeavouring to crush the Waldenses,
and in the latter city eighty persons were
committed to the flames.

These measures were, however, quite in-
significant, compared with the bloody edicts,
and their barbarous execution, which speedi-
ly followed, for the annihilation of the true
people of God.   Innocent III. who ascended

the pontifical throne in the year 1192, watched over the Waldenses with a jealous eye,
and being destitute alike of justice and of
pity, he determined to punish, in the most
summary manner, all who held opinions different from those of the Romish church.   He
accordingly charged his ministers to burn the
leaders, to disperse the flocks, and to confis
cate the property of every one who did not
implicitly believe in all the sayings of that
apostate church; in consequence of which,
many of the Waldensian pastors perished in
the flames at Nevers, and other places of
France, in 1198, and the years following.

   The province of Narbonne was particularly
the object of Innocent's attention.   In 1193,
he sent into it Guy and Regnier, two monks
of Citeaux, who may be considered as having
laid the foundation of the *inquisition*.   Their
commission was to discover and pursue heresy, being invested for that purpose with all
the authority of the Holy see.   Regnier was
subsequently appointed the Pope's legate;
but having fallen sick, Innocent joined to him
Peter of Castelnau, " whose zeal," says Sismondi, " more furious than that of his predecessors, is worthy of those sentiments, which
the very name of the inquisition inspires.—
The mission of the pope's commissaries or inquisitors," continues the same author, " was
not, however, limited to scrutinizing the

consciences of the heretics, confiscating their property, banishing, or sending them to the stake; they traversed the province, accompanied by a number of friars, who arrived successively to their aid; they preached and disputed against those who had wandered from the faith; and especially, when the lord of the place favoured the new opinions, not being able to employ force, they had recourse to the power of their disputations."

About the year 1204, two new orders of regulars were instituted, namely, those of St. Dominic and St. Francis. To the first of these falsely denominated *saints*, the erection of that horrid court, the inquisition, is ascribed.

This iniquitous court soon extended its authority, and enlarged the number of its tribunals in every kingdom of Europe, where any of the people were suspected of heresy. Every where its progress was marked with blood. Racks, dungeons, and flames, awaited the miserable beings who were dragged within its walls; and, under the cloak of religion, all the malice and ingenuity of hell were manifested by its supporters, in their barbarous proceedings towards their unhappy victims.*

---

* "The form of proceeding of the inquisitors, is an infallible way to destroy whomsoever the inquisitors wish. The prisoners are not confronted with the ac-

The Waldenses were the first objects of
inquisitorial cruelty.   By the aid of the civil
power, multitudes of them were put to the
most cruel deaths, for their steadfast adhe-
rence " to the word of God, and the testimony

cuser or informer.   Nor is there any informer, or
witness, who is not listened to.   A public convict, a
notorious malefactor, an infamous person, a child, are
in the holy office, though no where else, credible accusers and witnesses.   Even the son may depose
against the father, the wife against her husband.
This procedure, unheard of till the institution of this
court, makes the whole kingdom tremble.   Suspicion
reigns in every breast.   Friendship and quietness are
at an end.   The brother dreads his brother, the father
the son."—In addition to the judges, (often the most
abandoned of characters,) whose number generally
was three, and who are called *Lords of the Inquisition*,
there were many *Familiars*, who mingled in all socie-
ties, and acted the part of spies and informers.   No
person durst open his mouth against this court, as he
knew not but some of the familiars might give information, and the officers of the inquisition drag him
within the walls of their prison, from which few ever
returned.   Such, indeed, was the terror which this
court inspired, that parents delivered up their children, and husbands their wives, to be conveyed to its
dungeons, without daring to murmur, lest they should
share a similar fate.   All who were imprisoned by
this tribunal, were given up as dead; for although
they might be perfectly innocent, yet the inquisitors
seldom permitted any to pass without the walls of
their prison, lest they should make known to the people the deeds of darkness which were practised in
these habitations of horrid cruelty.

of Christ." Notwithstanding all the efforts of the Papal see, however, the heresy of the Vaudois remained as far as ever from being subdued. Enraged at thus being unable to destroy the enemies of the church, by the engines already in operation, the blood-thirsty Pope had recourse to another and a more summary method of exterminating a people, of whom it may truly be said, " the world was not worthy." This was nothing less than open war, to assist in which, all the Romish princes and nobles were invited to take up arms, and abbots and priests were commissioned to preach throughout Christendom a crusade against the Albigenses. These heralds of cruelty promised paradise, and the remission of sins, to all who should take the cross in this *holy* war, and serve against the Albigenses for forty days; together with the utmost extent of indulgence, which former Popes had granted to those who laboured for the deliverance of the holy land.

To preserve some appearance of decency, however, the court of Rome pretended that nothing would give the church greater satisfaction, than the prevention of bloodshed, provided the heretics could be reclaimed by persuasion. Relying too implicitly on these assurances, the Albigenses proposed to hold a public conference with their opponents, where the points in dispute might be discussed

by an appeal to Scripture, on condition that
the business should be conducted with im-
partiality and propriety. For the sake of
amusing the Albigenses till their own plans
were ripe for execution, the bishops acceded
to the proposal, and the conference took
place in 1206 near Carcassone. But while
the parties were engaged in dispute, the army
of the Crusaders advanced, and decided the
controversy, according to the custom of the
Romish church, by the slaughter of an immense number of these unsuspecting people.

Raymond VI. Count of Toulouse, and several others of the French nobility, having
afforded protection to the Albigenses, multitudes of these persecuted Christians took up
their residence in the country of Toulouse.
Raymond's conduct, however, gave great of-
fence to the sovereign Pontiff, and Innocent
evinced the utmost solicitude to prevail upon
him to expel the heretics from his dominions.
For this purpose he sent his legate, Peter of
Castelnau, to the count, requiring him to
sign a treaty, by which the united forces of
the Roman catholics were to be employed in
their extermination. But all his entreaties
to induce Raymond to banish so great a number of his peaceable subjects, to persecute
them, or to admit into his state an army that
was to pillage or kill all those whom the
priests should point out as heretics, proving

fruitless, Castelnau excommunicated Raymond, and laid his country under an interdict. Innocent lost no time in confirming the sentence of excommunication, which had been pronounced by his legate. He even wrote himself to the count, on the 20th May 1207, beginning his letter in these haughty terms:—"If we could open your heart, we should find, and would point out to you, the detestable abominations that you have committed; but as it is harder than the rock, it is in vain to strike it with the words of salvation: we cannot penetrate it. Pestilential man! what pride has seized your heart, and what is your folly, to refuse peace with your neighbours, and to brave the divine laws, by protecting the enemies of the faith? If you do not fear eternal flames, ought you not to dread the temporal chastisements which you have merited by so many crimes?"

Alarmed at these menaces, Raymond at length consented to purchase peace with his enemies, by engaging to exterminate the Albigenses from his states; but Peter of Castelnau, judging that he did not proceed in the work with adequate zeal, met the count at St. Giles, and, after reproaching him with perjury, with being a favourer of heretics, and a tyrant, he again pronounced on him the sentence of excommunication. One of Raymond's adherents, who was present at this

violent scene, having met Castelnau, on the
15th of January, 1208, at the side of the
Rhone, entered into a dispute with him respecting heresy and its punishments.   Castelnau answered him in language so menacing
and insulting, that, already irritated by the
quarrel with his lord, and now feeling himself personally offended, stabbed him with his
poignard, and fled from the country.

The intelligence of this assassination filled
Innocent with the most ungovernable rage;
and though Raymond protested his own innocence, and even exerted himself to the utmost
to apprehend the assassin, yet his Holiness
immediately published a bull, in which he declared that it was the devil who had instigated his principal minister, Raymond, count of
Toulouse, against the legate of the Holy see.
He laid under an interdict all the places
which should afford a refuge to the murderers of Castelnau; he demanded that the count
should be publicly anathematized in all the
churches: "And as," he added, "following
the canonical sanctions of the holy fathers,
that *we must not observe faith towards those
who keep not faith towards God,* or who are
separated from the communion of the faithful, we discharge, by apostolic authority, all
those who believe themselves bound towards
this count, by any oath, either of alliance or
of fidelity; we permit every catholic man, to

pursue his person, to occupy and retain his territories, *especially for the purpose of exterminating heresy.*"

Raymond, naturally mild and timid, was exceedingly desirous of saving himself and his subjects from the fury of their enemies; and, taking along with him his nephew, Raymond Roger, he went to Arnold, Abbot of Citeaux, whom the Pope had made leader of the crusade, in order if possible to avert the threatened storm. Arnold received them in a most haughty manner, and after carelessly listening to their protestations of innocence, and their petition to be heard before they were condemned, he told them, that if they wished to obtain any mercy, they must address themselves to the Pope. Raymond Roger immediately perceived there was no alternative but to arm themselves in their own defence; but his uncle, petrified with terror, offered to submit to any conditions, rather than draw the crusaders into his states. He accordingly agreed to make common cause with that fanatical army in their efforts to exterminate the heretics, to surrender to them seven of his castles as a pledge of his sincerity, and to submit to whatever judgment the legate should be pleased to pronounce upon him. After making these concessions, he was conducted into the church of St. Giles, with a cord about his neck, and his shoulders

naked, and there severely scourged with a
whip; and then, as a matter of favour, he
was allowed to take the cross against the
heretics.

Raymond Roger, on the other hand, was
more bold and determined, and instead of
yielding an implicit obedience to the orders
of the court of Rome, he retired into his
states, and immediately commenced preparations for resisting the attacks of his enemies.
His uncle Raymond VI. who had been compelled to agree to lead the army of the crusaders against him, was so overwhelmed with
grief at this part of the stipulation with the
legate, that he solicited leave to take a jour-
ney to Rome, for the purpose of humbling
himself before the sovereign Pontiff. This
request could not be denied; and the count
left the army, choosing any degradation which
might be put on himself, rather than continue
with it, "to be a spectator of the murder of
thousands of peaceable and virtuous men, and
the ruin of his own nephew."

In the meantime, the Popish army, consisting of upwards of a *hundred thousand* men,
entered the territories of Raymond Roger,
attacked the Albigenses, took possession of
their towns, filled the streets with slaughter
and blood, and precipitated multitudes of both
sexes, whom they had taken prisoners, into
the flames. But Raymond Roger had chiefly

calculated on the defence of his two great cities, Beziers and Carcassone; and having made provision in the former of these cities for repelling the attacks of the enemy, he took up his residence in the latter. When the crusaders arrived in the neighbourhood of Beziers, about the middle of July 1209, the fate of that city was easily foreseen. Sensible of the danger of his people, and grieved for the calamities which were ready to fall upon them, Raymond Roger hastened to the legate, and throwing himself at his feet, earnestly supplicated that the city might be spared, or at least that the innocent might not suffer indiscriminately with the guilty. To which the legate replied, that he must defend himself in the best way he could, for he should show him no mercy.

Finding the legate inflexible, the young viscount informed the inhabitants of his ill success, and of the only conditions upon which pardon could be obtained, namely, that all the Albigenses should either abjure their religion, or that they should be delivered into the hands of the popish army. To the first of these proposals only, the Roman catholic inhabitants of Beziers lent an ear, and used every entreaty with the Albigenses to induce them to submit to the religion of Rome. The latter, however, replied, "That they never could consent to purchase a

prolongation of the present perishing life,
at the price of renouncing their faith; that
they were fully persuaded God could, if he
pleased, protect and defend them; but they
were as fully persuaded, that if it were his
good pleasure to be glorified by the confession of their faith, it would be a high honour
conferred upon them to lay down their lives
for righteousness' sake; that they preferred
displeasing the Pope, who could only kill
their bodies, much more to incurring the displeasure of God, who could destroy both soul
and body at once; that they hoped never to
be ashamed of, nor forsake a faith by which
they had been taught the knowledge of Christ
and his righteousness, nor at the hazard of
eternal death, barter it for a religion which
annihilated the merits of the Saviour, and
rendered his righteousness of none effect.
They therefore left it to the Roman catholics
and the Viscount to make the best terms they
could for themselves, but entreated that they
would not promise any thing in *their* behalf
inconsistent with their duty as Christians."

The Roman catholic inhabitants next had
recourse to the legate, representing their uni-
form attachment to the Romish faith; but
that sanguinary ecclesiastic declared with an
oath, that unless every individual within the
walls of Beziers acknowledged his guilt, and
submitted to the judgment of the Holy see,

no mercy would be extended to any. Scarcely had this message been conveyed to the inhabitants, when orders were given to make
an assault upon the city. Resistance was
vain. The besiegers were immediately masters of Beziers, and a scene of bloodshed and
cruelty followed, of which the most unci-
vilized barbarians might have been ashamed.
As the murderers were entering the gates,
some of the knights inquired of the legate
how they should distinguish the catholics
from the heretics; to which Arnold instantly
replied, " *Kill them all,—the Lord will know
well those who are his.*" So dreadful was
the slaughter of the Albigenses on this occasion, that seven thousand dead bodies were
counted in one of the churches of the city,
and in all the others a spectacle equally lamentable was exhibited. When the murderers had completed their awful work, they set
fire to the city, and consumed it to ashes.
The number of victims who fell a prey at
that time to popish cruelty is differently
stated, some historians making it amount to
sixty thousand, while others reduce it to
twenty-three thousand; but which ever of
these numbers is correct, we see, in the
whole transaction, the " wrath of the dragon"
displayed in a manner the most fearful against
the seed of the church of Christ.

Still unsatiated with blood, the crusaders

proceeded to Carcassone, and sat down before that city on the 1st of August. This city was much stronger by nature than Beziers; its fortifications had been augmented, and it was defended by a numerous garrison. The popish army, however, was now increased to upwards of three hundred thousand men; and an attack having been made on one of the suburbs, after an obstinate resistance it was taken. The assailants then proceeded to the attack of the second suburb, but they were repulsed with very great loss. For eight days the besieged continued to defend it with success; but they at last evacuated it, and retired into the city.

The king of Arragon, who had lately joined the army of the crusaders, having offered himself as a mediator between the contending parties, the young Viscount readily accepted the proposal. But the legate, who was averse to any peace which should suspend the massacres, took care to propose conditions to which every generous mind would disdain to accede. These were, that Raymond Roger "might quit the city with twelve others, and that the remainder of the citizens and soldiers should be abandoned to his pleasure." "Rather than do what the legate demands of me," replied the viscount, "I would suffer myself to be flayed alive. He shall not have the least of my company at his mercy. I am re-

solved to defend both myself and my subjects
by every means that God has put in my
power."

No sooner had this message been returned
to the legate, than he gave orders to take the
city by assault. But, notwithstanding the
immense multitude which rushed forward to
the walls, and their vigorous efforts to render themselves masters of the place, the re-
pulse they met with from the besieged was so
determined, that they fell by thousands, and
the ditches which surrounded the city were
filled with their dead bodies. The attack
was many times renewed, but the assailants
were at last obliged to retreat with immense
loss. The period of forty days, besides, for
which the crusaders had enlisted, was now
finished, and multitudes of the legate's forces
abandoned the enterprise, and returned to
their own countries. Alarmed at these dis-
couraging symptoms, the legate had recourse
to a stratagem, so unworthy and perfidious,
that its only apology can be, that it was the
device of a *Romish ecclesiastic.* He employed
a gentleman related to the Viscount who happened to be with him, to enter into the city
and renew the negotiation. Raymond Roger himself was exceedingly desirous of an
honourable capitulation; and, having been persuaded by the gentleman to accompany him
to the legate, and obtaining at the same time,

both from Arnold and from the lords of the
army, the most complete guarantee for his
safety and liberty, which the crusaders subsequently confirmed by an oath, he impru-
dently quitted the city, attended by three
hundred knights, and arrived at the legate's
tent. After having nobly and powerfully defended his conduct, he declared that he
awaited Arnold's decision, and was ready to
hear the conditions he should propose for the
capitulation of the city. Deeply imbued with
the faithless spirit of his master, the legate
immediately told him, "that he was himself
a prisoner until the city was taken." Entreaties and remonstrances were of no avail.
Arnold ordered the young viscount and all
his knights to be arrested, and committed to
the custody of Simon, earl of Montfort.

By this base act of treachery, the legate
imagined he would strike terror into the minds
of the besieged, and force them to surrender.
But while they mourned over the fate of their
lord, Divine Providence delivered them from
falling into the hands of their blood-thirsty
foes. Some of the citizens were acquainted
with a subterraneaus passage, which led to
the castle of Caberet, about three leagues
from Carcassone; and during the night they
all escaped by this cavern, abandoning their
riches to the enemy. Having arrived at the
castle, they dispersed themselves through dif-

ferent parts of the country, betaking themselves to those cities, the majority of the inhabitants in which were Albigenses.

On the morning following, the crusaders were astonished at not seeing any person on the walls of the city, and some time elapsed ere they were convinced that it was entirely deserted. Having at length entered, the legate took possession of the spoil in the name of the Church, and forbade every person, under the severest penalty, to carry off the smallest part of the plunder. He was, however, extremely mortified at the flight of the Albigenses; and wishing at the same time to dissemble his own perfidy, he issued a proclamation, declaring that he had permitted the inhabitants to quit the city; but that the honour of the Church rendered it necessary, that an example should be made of some of them. In addition to the three hundred knights who had been imprisoned with the Viscount, a number of prisoners had been taken in the neighbouring country by the crusaders. Out of these, the legate chose four hundred and fifty persons, the majority of whom were burned, and the remainder hanged! Raymond Roger, too, was poisoned in prison not long afterwards.

The provinces which had been conquered by the legate were bestowed as a gift on Simon, Earl of Montfort, a person who was of a cruel and perfidious disposition, and a fanatic in religion. Having attacked, and taken a number of castles, Montfort put to death all the Albigenses who fell into his hands. He then turned his arms against .Albigeois, the dominions of Raymond Roger, Count of Foix, and soon obtained possession of several parts of that country, where cruelties equally revolting to humanity were committed on the unoffending people of God. But being at length deserted by numbers of the crusaders, who had become weary of so protracted a war, Montfort agreed to a treaty with the Count of Foix, which for a few weeks suspended the conflict, towards the close of the year 1209.

—••»•❺ ◉ ❺•••—

CHAPTER IV.

HAVING desolated a country which was considered the principal residence of the Albigenses, and massacred thousands of its inhabitants, we might have expected that the votaries of Rome would have been satiated with human blood. But it is long since the Spirit of inspiration predicted, that nothing less would serve the Popish Church, than being " *drunk* with the blood of the saints, and with the blood of the martyrs of Jesus."

It would be painful to enter into a detail of
the relentless barbarities and heart-rending
cruelties which, on the renewal of the war,
were committed on the Albigenses by the
Earl of Montfort. An outline only of a few
of his atrocities, and of the sufferings to which
he subjected those unoffending people, is all
that can be given here.

A fresh supply of crusaders having arrived
in the conquered provinces, to assist the Earl
of Montfort in exterminating the heretics, his
treaty with the Count of Foix was violated
very soon after it had been made. For some
time, however, the Earl, instead of adding to
his acquisitions, found himself deprived of a
number of places in the viscounties of Beziers
and Carcassone, of which he had already
taken possession. But new levies of crusaders daily arriving from the north of France,
where the monks had recommenced their
preaching, the haughty Earl set no bounds to
his ambition and cruelty. Having attacked
and carried several castles, all the inhabitants
in which were put to the sword, he laid siege,
in the beginning of June 1210, to Minerva, a
place strongly fortified by nature, and situated in the territory of Narbonne, on the confines of Spain. A great majority of the inhabitants of this castle were Albigenses, and so
completely had the Popish worship been disregarded in it, that Montfort himself declared

that "no mass had been sung in it for thirty
years." For seven weeks the besieged defended themselves with great valour; but on
the 22d of July the crusaders obtained possession of the place. Adding insult to cruelty,
the infamous Montfort, at the very time he
had given orders to collect an enormous
quantity of dry wood to burn the inhabitants,
sent a Popish ecclesiastic to offer pardon to
all who should embrace the Romish faith.
"Resisting, however, unto blood," the Albigenses unanimously exclaimed, "We have
renounced the Church of Rome; and neither
death nor life will make us abandon the opinions that we have embraced." Fire was
accordingly set to the pile, and by Montfort's
orders *one hundred and eighty men and
women* were committed to the flames. These
martyrs died stedfast in the truth, praising
God that he had counted them worthy to suffer death for their Redeemer's sake.

The crusaders next laid siege to Termes,
or Preissan, on the frontiers of Roussillon.
This castle was extremely strong, and commanded by Raymond of Termes, who for upwards of four months successfully repelled
the attacks of the enemy. Finding it, however, to be impossible longer to defend the
place, the inhabitants abandoned it on the
morning of the 23d of November, and fled to
the mountains; but being pursued by the

greater part of the Popish army, many of them were overtaken and killed on the spot. The siege of the castle of La Vaur followed the taking of Termes. After sustaining a siege of six months, this strongly fortified place was taken by assault on the 3d of May 1211; "and the only care of the Earl of Montfort was, to prevent the crusaders from instantly falling upon the inhabitants, and to beseech them rather to make prisoners, *that the priests of the living God might not be deprived of their promised joys!!*" "Very soon," adds a monkish writer, who was an eye-witness of the whole transaction, "they dragged out of the castle Aimery, lord of Montreal, and other knights to the number of eighty. The noble Count (Montfort) immediately ordered them to be hanged upon the gallows; but as soon as Aimery, the stoutest among them, was hanged, the gallows fell; for, in their great haste, they had not well fixed it in the earth. The Count, seeing that this would produce great delay, ordered the rest to be massacred; and the pilgrims, receiving the order with the greatest avidity, very soon massacred them all upon the spot. The lady of the castle, who was sister to Aimery, and an execrable heretic, was, by the Count's order, thrown into a pit, which was filled up with stones; afterwards, our pilgrims collected the innumerable heretics

that the castle contained, *and burned them
alive with the utmost joy!*"

. The success which attended the arms of
the crusaders filled the Count of Foix and the
Earl of Toulouse with alarm; and having collected a considerable force, these two noble-
men not only checked the career of the Earl
of Montfort, but soon stripped him of the
greater part of his conquests. In a general
engagement, however, which took place at
Muret, near the Garonne, on the 12th of September, 1213, they were completely defeated;
and the crusaders, pursuing their victory, put
to the sword, or drowned in the Garonne, the
greater part of the opposing army.

Sismondi has thus traced the total ex-
tinction of the first reformation:—" The
slaughter, had been so prodigious, the massacres so universal, the terror so profound,
and of so long duration, that the Popish
Church appeared to have completely obtained
her object. The worship of the reformed
Albigenses had every where ceased. All
teaching was become impossible. Almost all
the doctors of the new Church had perished
in a frightful manner; and the very small
number of those who had succeeded in es-
caping the crusaders, had sought an asylum
in the most distant regions, and were able to
avoid new persecutions, only by preserving
the most absolute silence respecting their doc-

trines and their ancient destinies. The private
believers, who had not perished by the fire
and the sword, or who had not withdrawn by
flight from the scrutiny of the inquisition,
knew that they could only save their lives
by burying their secret in their own bosoms.
For them there were no more sermons, no
more prayers, no more Christian communion,
no more instructions. The triumph appeared
so complete, that the persecutors, in the con-
fidence of their victory, became divided, made
war reciprocally against each other, and were
ruined. But this momentary interruption to
the persecution served only to render it the
more destructive. The momentary toleration
in Albigeois recalled thither the preachers
who had escaped the first massacre, and involved them all in a second."

The Earl of Toulouse and his son Raymond
having raised an army for the recovery of
their dominions from the Earl of Montfort,
not only prosecuted the war with success, but
actually recovered Toulouse, the capital of
the country. While Montfort was endeavouring to retake that city, he was killed by
a stone thrown from the wall, in consequence
of which Amaury, Montfort's son, was obliged
to raise the siege, on the 25th of July 1218.

Favouring the pretensions of Amaury to
retain possession of the countries which his
father had conquered, Honorius III., who had

succeeded Innocent III. in the Papal See,
directed that another crusade should be form
ed against the Albigenses.   For this purpose
he sent the following rescript into every province of France:—" We excommunicate all
heretics of both sexes, and of whatsoever sect,
with their favourers, receivers, and defenders;
and, moreover, all those who cause any edicts
or customs contrary to the liberty of the
Church to be observed, unless they remove
them from their public records in two months
after the publication of this sentence.   Also
we excommunicate the makers and writers
of those statutes, and moreover, all governors,
consuls, rulers, and counsellors of places
where such statutes and customs shall be published and kept, and all those who shall pre-
sume to pass judgment, or to publish such
judgments as shall be made according to
them."   Honorius also wrote to Louis VII.
king of France, exhorting that monarch to
take up arms in defence of the Church.   "It
is the command of God," said his Holiness,
" who says, If thou shalt hear say in any one
of thy cities which the Lord thy God hath
given thee to dwell there, saying, Let us go
and serve other gods, which ye have not
known, thou shalt smite the inhabitants of
that city with the edge of the sword."—It is
worthy of remark here, that the ambitious and
perfidious Roman Pontiffs, and their no less

perfidious supporters, uniformly use, and grossly pervert, the words of Scripture to sanction their most detestable and bloody deeds, "One would imagine," says a late writer, "that they had only studied the Bible to make sacrilegious applications of it."

Louis, who did not yield in fanaticism, or in hatred against the Albigenses, to any of the monks, immediately began to collect an army of crusaders, at the head of which he placed himself, and joined Amaury, in 1219, in besieging the castle of Marmande. After holding out for some time, the besieged offered to surrender, provided they were granted their lives. "I will receive you to mercy," replied Louis, "and suffer you to go away, carrying only your bodies with you." These conditions being of course accepted, the gates of the place were thrown open to the crusaders; but instead of fulfilling their agreement with the inhabitants, the Bishop of Saintes advised Louis "immediately to kill and burn them as heretics." His advice was, alas! but too implicitly followed, for all the inhabitants, men, women, and children, to the number of five thousand, were massacred!

The crusaders next bent all their forces against Toulouse, before which Louis arrived on the 16th of June. The Pope's legate had sworn, "That in the said Toulouse should remain neither man, woman, boy, nor girl,

but that all should be put to death, without
sparing old or young; and that in all the city
there should not remain one stone above another, but all should be demolished and thrown
down." The besieged, however, defended
themselves with so much bravery, and so successfully repelled the assaults of the enemy,
that Louis was compelled to raise the siege
on the 1st of August, and to retire with pre-
cipitation.

For some time the absurd project of a new
crusade to the holy land, engaged the attention of the Court at Rome, and suspended
the war against the Albigenses. That crusade, however, being at length abandoned, a
new one was formed against the already
almost annihilated opponents of the Popish
Church. On the 6th of June 1226, accordingly, Louis VIII. of France, arrived at Avignon, with an army of fifty thousand horsemen.
For three months the besieged defended the
city with the greatest bravery, during which
time thousands of the French army perished
in the conflict. Disease and famine, besides,
raged in so fearful a manner among the crusaders, that Matthew Paris, the monk of St.
Albans, makes the number of those who
perished while prosecuting this siege, amount
to twenty thousand men. Despairing of re-
ducing the city by force, the Pope's legate,
as usual, had recourse to fraud; and having

given his oath that he only wished their wel-
fare, the citizens consented, on the 12th of
September, to receive him and the lords of
the army within their walls, for the purpose
of finally adjusting the terms of the capitulation. But no sooner had they opened their
gates, than the whole army of the crusaders
rushed forward, and, seizing the inhabitants,
they bound them in chains, plundered their
houses, put numbers of them to death, and
demolished the towers and walls of the city.

Thus, after nearly thirty years of cruel persecution, the Albigenses were almost either
wholly destroyed,* or driven from their country. During all that period blood never ceased
to flow, nor the flames to devour their victims,
in Albigeois and the surrounding country;
and the few who escaped the edge of the
sword fled for refuge to the valleys of Piedmont, or took up their abode in Austria,
Bohemia, and other kingdoms to which the
horrors of persecution had not yet extended.

But besides those who fell in war, or were
murdered by the crusaders, that horrid engine
of Popish cruelty, the inquisition, was continually at work, making fearful havoc among
the disciples of Christ.. From 1206 to 1228,
the numbers which were apprehended were

---

* It is computed that upwards of a million of the
Albigenses perished, within three years, by the hands
of the crusaders.

so immense, that, in the latter year, the Arch·
bishops of Aix, Arles, and Narbonne, found
it necessary to intercede with the inquisitors,
to defer for a little their work of imprison·
ment, until the Pope should be apprised of
the numbers already confined, it being im
possible to procure a sufficient quantity of
materials to build prisons in which to contain
them. ' But these courts were not content
with *imprisoning* heretics; the rack and the
flames were daily employed, as the most summary methods of ridding themselves of all
who had incurred their diabolical vengeance.

To render this horrid court permanent, and
to subject it wholly to the power of the ecclesiastics, a Council was assembled at Toulouse, in 1229. After agreeing on the manner
in which heretics who fell into their hands were
to be treated, that infamous assembly decreed
that the people should be prohibited from
reading the Bible. "We prohibit," says
the 14th canon, "laymen from having the
books of the Old and New Testaments; only
they who out of devotion desire it, may have
a psalter, a breviary, or the Hours of the
blessed Mary; *but we forbid them, in the most
express manner, to have the above-mentioned
books translated into the vulgar tongue.*" It
is true that, *indirectly,* the Church of Rome
had for a long time acted up to the spirit of
this canon; but this appears to be the first

instance of a *direct* prohibition of the people
reading the word of God. " What an honour,"
says Milner, " was this canon to the cause
of the Albigenses! What a confession of
guilt on the side of the Romanists! The people of God were thus, at length, for the most
part, exterminated in Toulouse, and found no
other resource than, by patient continuance in
well-doing, to commit themselves to their God
and Saviour. Antichrist, for the present,
was visibly triumphant in the south-west
parts of France, and the witnesses, ' clothed
in sackcloth,' there consoled themselves with
the hope of heavenly rest, being deprived of
all prospect of earthly enjoyments."

Although Raymond and other powerful
chiefs strongly protected their Waldensian
subjects, it does not appear that any of them
either understood or embraced their principles. Political motives, mixed no doubt with
feelings of commiseration for a people who
were harmless, peaceable, and loyal, induced
these princes to unite in endeavouring to defend the Albigenses from the arms of the crusaders. But being Roman Catholics, they
frequently suffered themselves to become the
dupes of the Papal see; and hence they were
at length made to feel, that, notwithstanding
all their submissions, the very " tender mercies" of the Roman Pontiff and of his emissaries, were cruel.

But though the greater number of the Albigenses in France had perished, and though those of them who escaped had been driven into exile, yet their doctrines were as far as ever from being eradicated. Their dispersion scattered throughout Europe those sparks of divine truth, which the inquisitors still laboured to extinguish, and the Court of Rome beheld with alarm the rays of light bursting through the gloom which it imagined had been rendered every where impenetrable. Even in Rome itself, the sovereign Pontiff, Gregory IX. found himself surrounded with heretics; but instead of being convinced of the utter absurdity of attempting to control the consciences of men, and to compel them to receive a rule of faith which they justly regarded as being founded on falsehood and error, he had recourse to the same unhallowed methods that had been used by his predecessors, of supporting the pretensions of the Papacy to inculcate uniformity of sentiment throughout Christendom.

Numbers of the Waldenses were accordingly burned in the city of Rome, in 1231; and in 1232, Gregory wrote to the Emperor Frederick II. informing him, "That the Catharines, Paterines, poor of Lyons, and other heretics, formed in the school of the Albigenses, had appeared in Lombardy and the two Sicilies," and soliciting from him an

edict for their destruction. With this request
the Emperor complied, and " commanded all
judges immediately to deliver to the flames
every man who should be convicted of heresy
by the bishop of his diocess, and to pull out
the tongue of those to whom the bishop should
think it proper to show favour, that they might
not corrupt others."

The flames of persecution were not, however, confined to Italy. In Arragon the inquisition was introduced, in 1232, and for a
century and a half made fearful havoc among
the Waldenses, till at length there were none
of them left in that kingdom. In Poland,
Spain, the Netherlands, Germany, and other
countries, the same atrocities were committed;
and, in short, wherever a professor of the
Waldensian faith could be found, the adherents of Rome thought it a meritorious service
to bathe their hands in his blood!

CHAPTER V.

WHILE the Albigenses in France were exposed to all the horrors of persecution, the
Waldenses in the valleys of Piedmont enjoyed a considerable portion of tranquillity. Numerous efforts, it is true, were made by the
emissaries of Rome, to induce the dukes of

Savoy to destroy the inhabitants of these valleys; but for upwards of two centuries, these
princes resisted all their solicitations to persecute their loyal and peaceable subjects.
Under the protection of the dukes, therefore,
the Waldenses remained for several ages in
comparative tranquillity. Their light continued all that time to shine amidst the darkness which surrounded them; and although
the inquisitors frequently dragged several of
them to the stake, yet no open attack was
made on their country till the year 1400.

In that year, however, a violent outrage
was committed on those who inhabited the
valley of Pragela. Their invaders chose the
month of December, when the mountains were
covered with snow, for accomplishing their
horrid work; when, falling unexpectedly on
these peaceable people, they put many of them
to the sword, and took possession of their
caves. Those who escaped this massacre,
fled to the highest mountains of the Alps, the
mother carrying the cradle in the one hand,
and in the other leading those little children
who were able to walk. Pursued by their
persecutors, many of them were overtaken
and murdered, without respect to age or sex,
while those who avoided the sword of their
enemies were either starved to death, or
perished among the snow. Eighty children
were next morning discovered bereft of life,

having fallen a prey to the inclemency of the season; many of the mothers were lying at their side, while others were found in the very agonies of death! Of the few who escaped, some fled to Calabria, and others sought an asylum in Provence, whither they were pursued by the cruel hand of persecution.—This outrageous attack made a deep and lasting impression on the minds of the Vaudois; and although a season of some repose followed, yet "for more than a century afterwards, they were wont to speak of it as of a dreadful scene which was still present to their view; and from generation to generation, they continued to relate, with deep impressions of horror, that sudden surprise which had occasioned so much affliction and calamity among them."

In 1487, the Pope issued a rigorous bull against the Waldenses, and commissioned Albert, Archdeacon of Cremona, as his legate, to carry his bloody purpose into effect:—"We have heard," said he, with much displeasure, that certain sons of iniquity, followers of that abominable and pernicious sect of malignant men, who are called the poor people of Lyons, or the Waldenses, who have long ago endeavoured in Piedmont, and other neighbouring parts, by the instigation of him who is the sower of evil works, through by-ways, purposely sought out, and hidden precipices,

to ensnare the sheep belonging to God, and
at last to bring them to the perdition of their
souls by deadly cunning, are damnably risen
up under a feigned pretence of holiness, being
led into a reprobate sense, and do greatly err
from the way of truth.—If you shall think
it expedient, to cause, exhort, and induce all
the faithful in those parts, by fit preachers of
God preaching the cross or the crusade, to
fight manfully against the same heretics,
having taken the saving sign of the cross upon
their hearts and garments; and to grant such
as are signed with the cross, and fight against
the said heretics, or such as contribute thereunto, may obtain, according to your appoint-
ment, once in their life, and also at the point
of death, a plenary indulgence and remission
of all their sins."

No sooner had Albert received this infamous commission, than he proceeded with the
French king's lieutenant, and a body of troops,
to the valley of Loyse. Aware of his approach, the inhabitants fled to their caves at
the top of the mountains, carrying with them
their children, and what was thought necessary for their support. The lieutenant immediately went in search of their places of
retreat, which having found, he caused great
quantities of wood to be placed at the entrance
of the caves, and set on fire. The consequence was, that four hundred infants were

suffocated in their cradles, or in the arms of their also deceased mothers, while multitudes were either precipitated over the rocks and dashed in pieces, or slaughtered by the brutal soldiery. Upwards of three thousand of the inhabitants of this valley perished on that occasion; and so effectually was the work of destruction accomplished, that it was afterwards peopled with entirely new inhabitants.

Still thirsting for blood, the inhuman Albert marched against the inhabitants of the Piedmontese valleys, in 1488, at the head of an army of eighteen thousand men. In order more effectually to accomplish his purpose, he divided his army into three detachments, and marched in different directions against Angrogna, Lucerna, and the other valleys, thus almost encompassing the Vaudois on every side. Availing themselves, however, of the advantages of their situation, the inhabitants defended the passes of the mountains with so much vigour, that their invaders were defeated, and forced to retreat with great loss. During this conflict, the women and children were entreating the Lord, on their knees, to protect his persecuted people.

Convinced that his Waldensian subjects had always been a loyal and obedient people, Philip VII. Duke of Savoy, was touched with compassion for their sufferings. But having been informed that their young children were monsters, he ordered some of them to be brought before him at Pignerol, where being satisfied of the false statements and deadly malice of their adversaries, the Popish priests, he blamed himself for being so easily imposed upon by their slanderous reports, and declared it to be his resolution henceforward to grant protection to the inhabitants of the valleys. He felt himself utterly unable, however, to carry his kind intentions into effect. The inquisitors continued daily to apprehend, and deliver over to the secular power for punishment, great numbers of the Vaudois; and so dreadful were the cruelties which were committed on these servants of Christ, and so great was their constancy amidst their most excruciating torments, that the persecutions of the first ages of Christianity, and the memory of the primitive martyrs, seemed to be revived. We shall notice only one instance among many which might be given. A Waldensian pastor, named Catelin Girard, while standing on the block on which he was to be burned, requested his executioners to give him two stones. This request being with some difficulty complied with, the martyr, holding them in his hands, exclaimed, "Sooner shall I eat these stones, than you shall be able to put an end to that religion for which you put me to death;" and throwing them on the ground, he calmly submitted to the stroke of death.

In this manner the Papal inquisitors continued to harass and persecute the Waldenses, till 1532, in consequence of which, they had been obliged for several years to assemble for the worship of God in private. In that year, however, they mustered up more courage, and unterrified "by the fury of the oppressor," resolved to re-open their churches and openly to preach the gospel. This decisive avowal of their principles increased the indignation of the Romish priests; and, instigated by them, the Duke of Savoy issued an order to invade and plunder their country. Five hundred men, accordingly, entered the valleys, at a time when the inhabitants were completely off their guard, and laid waste every inch of ground within their reach. Instead, however, of being able to accomplish their purpose, of putting the Waldenses to the sword, these invaders were at first successfully resisted; and the inhabitants gathering courage and increasing in numbers, the assailants were compelled at length to evacute the country with the loss of a considerable number of their troops. Perceiving how preposterous it was to attempt the subjugation of Piedmont by an armed force, their strong holds in the mountains affording the Vaudois a safe retreat,

until the fury of persecution had exhausted
itself, the Duke of Savoy relinquished the
prosecution of open war, and suffered the
inquisitors to destroy, by a slower process,
all who fell into their hands.

The Waldenses, however, defended themselves with so much courage and success, that
the priests were at length compelled to leave
the country; the mass was expelled from
Piedmont; and at the commencement of the
sixteenth century, they not only enjoyed a
considerable portion of tranquillity, but a
great increase had been made to their numbers,
The Reformation from Popery, which was
accomplished at that period, through the instrumentality of Zuinglius, Luther, Melanc-
thon, and others, was hailed with joy by the
Waldenses; and a friendly intercourse was
immediately commenced, and uniformly kept
up, between them and the Reformers.

Some of the Waldensian pastors, of Provence, wrote to Œcolampadius, about the
year 1530, for advice respecting the compli-
ance of several of their flocks with the un-
scriptural practices of their Roman Catholic
neighbours.* To this communication, the

* The reader is requested to observe that the correspondence which took place at this time between
the Waldenses and Œcolampadius, had no connection
with those in the valleys of Piedmont. It referred
solely to those in France. Those intrepid followers

Swiss Reformer returned the following remonstrance, which, for its sound and scriptural reasoning, deserves a place here.

" Œcolampadius wishes the grace of God, through Christ Jesus his Son, and the Holy Spirit, to his well-beloved brethren in Christ, called *Waldenses*.

" I have heard, that from fear of persecution, you dissemble and conceal your faith; that you communicate with unbelievers; and that you attend abominable mass. Now with the heart we believe unto righteousness, and with the mouth confession is made unto salvation. But those who are afraid to confess Christ before the world, shall find no acceptance with God; for our God is truth; and as he is a jealous God, he cannot endure that any of his servants should take upon them the yoke of Antichrist. For there is no fellowship or communion between Christ and Belial; and if you communicate with unbelievers, by going to their abominable masses, you will there hear blasphemies against the death and sufferings of Christ. For when they boast,

of the Lamb, the Piedmontese, were never guilty of compromising their principles. They resisted even unto blood; and submitted to be "tortured, not accepting deliverance," that they might preserve the faith in its purity, and " have no fellowship whatever with the works of darkness."

that by means of such sacrifices they make
satisfaction to God for the sins both of the
living and the dead, what naturally follows,
but that Christ, by his death, has not made
sufficient expiation, and consequently that
Christ is not a Saviour, and that he died for
us in vain! If we participate in that impure
table, we declare ourselves to be of one and
the same body with the wicked, however contrary we may pretend it to be to our wills
and inclinations. And when we say *Amen*
to their prayers, do we not deny Christ?

  "What death ought we not to undergo,—
what torture and torment ought we not to endure,—nay, into what abyss of woe and misery ought we not to plunge ourselves, rather
than by our presence to testify our consent
to, and approbation of, the blasphemies of the
wicked. I know that your infirmity is great.
But those who have been taught that they
were redeemed by the blood of Christ, ought
to be courageous, and always to stand in awe
of Him who can cast both soul and body into
hell. And what? is it enough for us to have
preserved this life alone? Shall this be more
precious to us than that of Christ? And are
we satisfied with having enjoyed the delights
and pleasures of this perishing world? Are
there not crowns laid before us, and shall we
flinch and recoil? Who will believe that our
faith was true and sincere, if it want zeal

and ardour in the time of persecution? I beseech the Lord to increase your faith.

"Surely it is better for us to lose our lives than to be overcome by temptations. And, therefore, I beseech you thoroughly to consider this matter; for if it be lawful for us to conceal our faith under the tyranny of Antichrist, it must be lawful for us to do so under that of the Turk; or you might worship, with Diocletian, at the altars of Jupiter or Venus; and what then will become of our faith towards God? If we do not give to God that honour which is his due, and if our lives be nothing but dissimulation and hypocrisy, he will spue us out of his mouth. How shall we glorify God amidst sufferings and tribulations, if we deny him? When once we have put our hand to the plough, we must not, brethren, look back; nor must we yield to the dictates and instigations of the flesh, which, by prompting us to sin, though it may endure many things which are distressing in this world, may at last suffer shipwreck in the haven."

This letter came at a very seasonable time, as they to whom it was addressed were immediately called upon to carry its principles into effect.

Instigated by the Pope's nuncio, Francis I. the French monarch, in 1540, put his signa-

ture to an edict which threatened the total
destruction of the Waldenses throughout the
whole of his dominions. "It enacted, that
every dissentient from the holy mother church
should acknowledge his errors, and obtain
reconciliation within a stated period, under
the severest penalties in case of disobedience;
and because Merindol was considered to be
the principal seat of the heresy, that devoted
city was ordered to be razed to the ground.
With a species of the most refined cruelty,
the edict added, that all the caverns, hiding-
places, cellars, and vaults, in the vicinity of
the town, should be carefully examined and
destroyed, that the woods should be cut down,
and all the gardens and orchards laid waste,
and that none who had possessed a house or
property in Merindol, or within a certain distance, should ever occupy it again, either in
his own person, or in that of any of his name
or family, in order that the memory of the
excommunicated sect might be utterly wiped
away from the province, and the place be
made a desert. This horrible decree was
put into execution by an armed force, without
the least mercy or forbearance; the wretched
inhabitants fled *en masse*, and because they
refused to surrender themselves at discretion,
the commander of the troops which marched
against Merindol, threatened death, without

trial or appeal, to every one who should render them the least assistance. Nothing ever exceeded the dreadful scenes which followed."

The town of Coste was next assaulted and taken, when scenes of atrocity, the most detestable and villanous, were committed, the very recital of which would fill the mind of the reader with horror. "It was in this manner," says Gilly, "that plunder, carnage, and violation were spread from one end of Provence to another; Dauphiné and Languedoc experienced nearly the same horrors, and few were the Protestants who were spared, and fewer those who had the courage to acknowledge that they belonged to the proscribed party. There was, however, one illustrious champion left, Aymond de la Voye, whose name ought not to be forgotten. This brave and pious man boldly went from village to village, to confirm the wavering, and re-assure the hopeless, until at length he exposed himself to suspicion, and was carried before a tribunal which was sitting for the condemnation of heretics. The first question that was put to him, was intended to draw forth a disclosure that would lead to the apprehension of others.

"Who are your associates?"

"My associates are those who know and do the will of my heavenly Father, whether

they be nobles, merchants, peasants, or men
of any other condition."

"Who is the head of the church?"

"Jesus Christ."

"Is not the Pope the head of the church?"

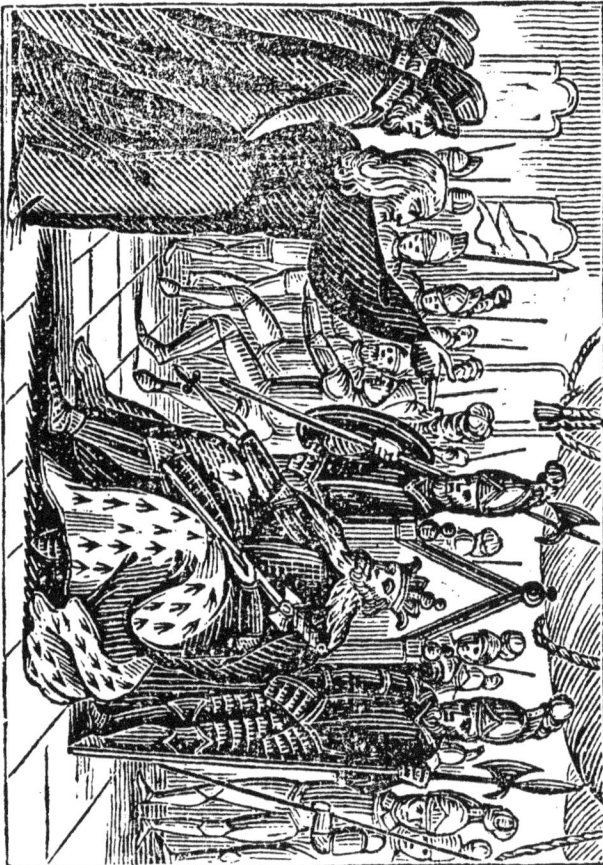

"No—if he is a good man, he is the minister and primate of the Roman church, but
nothing more."

"Is not the Pope the successor of St. Pe
ter?"

"Yes, if he be like St. Peter; but not
else."

His persecutors saw that he was not to be
moved, and ordered him to be led to execution. As he passed by an image of the Vir-
gin Mary, he refused to salute it; and the
execrations of an infuriated mob had no other
effect upon him, than to pray aloud, "Oh,
Lord, I beseech thee to make it known to
these deluded creatures, that it is to thee
only they are to bow the head, and offer
supplications." As he mounted the scaffold,
he cried out with a firm voice, "Be it known
that I die not a heretic, but a christian."
The clamorous multitude insisted that his
voice should be stopped; and, before the exe-
cutioner had inflicted the tortures usual upon
these occasions, an end was ordered to be put
to his existence, because there was no other
way of silencing the undaunted Aymond de
la Voye, whom even prolonged suffering could
not intimidate."

—◦◦◦●◉●◦◦◦—

CHAPTER VI.

THE dreadful sufferings of the Waldenses
in Provence deeply afflicted, and filled with

alarm, their brethren in the valleys of Piedmont. Similar barbarities continued to be
committed in various other places,* and they
knew not how soon an attack might be made
upon themselves. Nor were their fears
groundless. Francis I. having conquered
Piedmont, Paul III. who then filled the Papal throne, persuaded the parliament which
that monarch had assembled at Turin, vigor
ously to proceed against the Waldenses, as
" most pernicious heretics." The consequence was, that multitudes of the Vaudois
were seized and committed to the flames. In
vain did they petition the king to grant them
the same privileges under his government
which they and their forefathers had enjoyed
under the house of Savoy. Both Francis and
his parliament commanded them, under pain

* In Calabria especially, the Waldenses were subjected to the most cruel sufferings. A bull for their
extermination was issued by the Papal see, and no
mercy was shown to those who refused to be baptized
by a Romish priest. " The pastors were carried in
chains to Rome; some were starved to death in prison, others were tortured in the dungeons of the inquisition, after witnessing the utter destruction or
dispersion of their flock; and two were burnt at the
stake, to gratify the malignity of Pope Pius IV. who
could not be satisfied unless he saw with his own
eyes the expiring agonies of the heretics, who had
dared to question his infallibility." In short, the Waldenses of Calabria were *wholly exterminated.*

of death, to renounce their religion, and conform to the worship of the Popish church. The Waldenses, however, replied, "That in what regarded their religious worship, they could obey no commands which interfered with the laws of God, to whom they chose to be obedient in every thing that concerned his service, rather than to follow the fancies and inclinations of men."

The attention of Francis being engaged with a variety of other affairs, the destruction of the Waldenses was left to the inquisition. This unhallowed tribunal, ever alive to the perpetration of deeds of cruelty, exercised the commission which it had received with its usual barbarity. Numbers of the inhabitants of the valleys were unceasingly committed to the flames; and being seconded, in 1555, by the parliament of Turin, many of the most eminent of the Vaudois pastors perished within its walls, amidst the most excruciating tortures.

On the death of Francis, his son Henry II. was raised to the throne of France; and in 1559 Piedmont was again restored to Philibert Emanuel, duke of Savoy. Scarcely had this prince gained possession of the country of the Vaudois, than the monks of Pignerol earnestly entreated him to exterminate the inhabitants by means of the sword, and to people the valleys with the adherents of Rome

To avert, if possible, the danger with whicn they were threatened, the Waldenses pre·sented an humble petition to the duke, imploring his clemency. This paper shows so much firmness, mingled with Christian meekness, that, as a specimen of the numerous petitions which these persecuted people presented to their sovereigns, we shall give it entire.

" The humble supplication of the poor Waldenses, to the most serene, and high Prince, Philibert Emanuel, duke of Savoy, Prince of Piedmont, our most gracious lord.

"Festus, governor of Judea, being required by the chief priests and elders of the people to put to death the Apostle Paul, answered no less wisely than justly, that the Romans were not wont to put any to death before they had brought his accusers face to face, and given him time to answer for himself. We are not ignorant, most gracious prince, that many accusations are laid against us, and that many calumnies are cast upon us, to make us objects of abomination to all the Christians and monarchs in the Christian world. But if the Roman people, though pagans, were so equitable, as not to condemn any man before they knew and understood his reasons; and if the law condemns no man (as it is testified by Nicodemus, John vii) before he hath been heard, and before it is known what he hath done, the matter now in question being of so great concernment, namely, the glory of the most high God, and the salvation of so many souls, we do implore your clemency, most gracious prince, that you will be pleased to lend a willing ear to your poor subjects, in so just and righteous a cause.

"First, we do protest, before the Almighty and all-just God, before whose tribunal we must all one day appear, that we intend to live and die in the holy faith, piety, and religion of our Lord Jesus Christ; and that we do abhor all heresies, that have been, and are, condemned by the word of God.

"We do embrace the most holy doctrine of the prophets and apostles, as likewise of the Nicene and Athanasian creeds; we subscribe to the four councils, and to all the ancient fathers, in all such things as are not repugnant to the analogy of faith.

"We do most willingly yield obedience to our superiors; we ever endeavour to live peaceably with our neighbours; we have wronged no man, though provoked; nor do we fear that any can, with reason, complain against us.

"Finally, we never were obstinate in our opinions, but rather tractable, and always ready to receive all holy and pious admoni-

tions, as appears by our confessions of faith.
And we are so far from refusing a discus-
sion, or rather a free council, wherein all
things may be established by the word of
God, that we rather desire the same with all
our hearts.

"We likewise beseech your highness to
consider, that this religion 'we profess, is not
ours only, nor hath it been invented by man
of late years, as it is falsely reported; but it
is the religion of our fathers, grandfathers,
and great grandfathers, and other yet more
ancient predecessors of ours, and of the
blessed martyrs, confessors, prophets, and
apostles; and if any can prove the contrary,
we are ready to subscribe thereunto. The
word of God shall not perish, but remain for
ever; therefore, if our religion be the true
word of God, as we are persuaded, and not
the invention of men, no human force shall be
able to extinguish the same.

"Your highness knows, that this very same
religion hath, for many ages past, been most
grievously persecuted in all places; but so far
from being abolished and rooted out thereby,
that it hath rather increased daily, which is a
certain argument, that this work and counsel
is not the work of men, but of God, and
therefore cannot be destroyed by any violence. Therefore, we beseech your most
serene highness to consider, what it is to

undertake any thing against God, that so you may not imbrue your hands in innocent blood! Jesus is our Saviour; we will religiously obey all your highness's edicts, as far as conscience will permit; but when conscience says nay, your highness knows, we must rather obey God than man. We unfeignedly confess, that we ought to give to Cæsar that which belongs to Cæsar, provided we give also to God what is due to him.

" There want not those who will endeavour to incite the generous mind and courage of your highness, to persecute our religion by force of arms. But, O magnanimous prince, you may easily conjecture to what end they do it, that it is not out of zeal to God's glory, but rather to preserve their own worldly dignities, pomp, and riches; therefore we beseech your highness not to regard or countenance their sayings.

" The Turks, Jews, Saracens, and other nations, though never so barbarous, are suffered to enjoy their own religion, and are constrained by no man to change their manner of living and worship; and we, who serve and worship in faith the true and almighty God, and one true and only Sovereign, the Lord Jesus, and confessing one God, and one baptism, shall not we be suffered to enjoy the same privileges?

" We humbly implore your highness's good-

ness, and that for our Lord and Saviour Jesus
Christ's sake, to allow unto us, your most
humble subjects, the most holy gospol of the
Lord our God, in its purity; and that we may
not be forced to do things against our consciences; for which we shall, with all our
hearts, beseech our almighty and all good
God, to preserve your highness in prosperity."

This touching appeal had no effect. Four
hundred men invaded the valley of Lucerna,
and put to death many of the inhabitants.
This was followed by the arrival of a regular
army, in 1560, under the command of the
Count de la Trinite, who immediately attacked the village of Angrogna, and committed
many outrages on the persons and property of
the Vaudois. About two hundred peasants,
armed with slings, was all the Waldensian
force which could be mustered at this time,
to contend with twelve hundred disciplined
soldiers. Yet, as " the race is often not to
the swift, nor the battle to the strong," these
peasants forced the Count to retreat with disgrace. Enraged at this defeat, he advanced
a second time, and was again repulsed with
the loss of seventy men, while that on the
side of the Waldenses amounted only to three.
Having received reinforcements from Spain,
which increased the number of his army to
seven thousand, the Count determined to
wreak his vengeance, not only on the little

band who had so successfully opposed him,
but on all the Waldenses in the surrounding
country. Aware of their inability to contend
with a force so superior, the peasants, with
their wives and children, and the whole population, retired to their natural and inaccessible fortifications in the mountains. The
Count attempted to follow them, "and for
four days made every effort to get possession
of the defiles. Two colonels, eight captains,
and four hundred men, fell in these desperate
assaults, without an inch of ground being
gained. On the fifth day a fresh attack was
made in three different quarters, with the
reserve, composed of some Spanish companies, but the post was not carried; and upon
the general commanding his troops to return
again to the charge, they refused to obey. At
the moment when they began to waver, the
Vaudois saw the opportunity, and made a
sortie, which produced a universal panic and
rout among the assailants." "In several
fights," says Scipio Lentulus, who was an
eye-witness of the contest, "nine hundred of
the enemies were slain, whereas on our side
hardly fifteen were wanting."

The signal defeat which the Duke's army
at this time sustained, induced that prince to
suspend hostilities. He required, however,
that the Vaudois should send deputies to apo-
logise for their having taken up arms against

the forces of their sovereign. On the arrival of deputies at Turin, Chassincourt, one of the courtiers, rudely addressed them in the following words:—" How dare such wretches as you treat with a prince against whom you have made war? or how can such poor ignorant shepherds, who deserve a gibbet for your folly, have the assurance to contest religious points with a great prince, advised by men of learning, and authorised in his belief by the whole world?"—" Sir," replied the most aged of the deputies, " it is the goodness of our prince who has called us, which gives us the assurance to appear before him. Our resistance has been just, since it was compulsory, and God has approved of it by the wonderful assistance he has afforded us. Nor have we fought for worldly wealth, but purely for conscience sake; and that, when we found our prince endeavouring to put an end to the true service of God, and actuated not by his own will (as we charitably believe,) but by that of others, while executing with regret the commands of the Pope. With respect to the simplicity with which you reproach us, God hath blessed it, since the most humble instruments are often the most agreeable to him, and he can elevate the most ignoble for his own good purposes. The counsels of the Spirit are sufficiently wise, the hearts *He* excites, sufficiently courageous, and the arms which *He* strengthens, vigorous enough. We are ignorant, and affect n o other eloquence than to pray with faith. As to the death with which you threaten us, the word of our Sovereign is dearer than our lives; at all events, he who has the fear of God in his heart, fears not death."

Struck with this noble reply, Chassincourt renounced the Romish, and embraced the Vaudois faith. Having, at the same time, interceded with the Duke in their behalf, that prince granted an edict in their favour, which confirmed to them all their privileges, and permitted them to enjoy, not only the free exercise of their religion, but commerce with all the surrounding states under his dominion.

This suspension of hostilities lasted for four years, and had not the emissaries of Rome prevailed over the Duke's inclination, a much longer period of repose might have been afforded to the inhabitants of Piedmont. But in 1565, a new edict was issued, "enjoining every subject throughout the dominions of the Duke of Savoy, not conforming to the Church of Rome, to appear before the magistrates of their several districts, within ten days, and there either declare their readiness to go to mass, or quit the country in two months." Grieved at the sufferings to which their brethren had already been subjected, and anxious to avert the storm which now threatened them, the Protestant princes of Germany, and especially the Elector Palatine, interceded with the Duke in their behalf. Their efforts were seconded by the Duchess, who appears to have been a humane, if not a pious princess; which made so deep an impression on the mind of the Duke, that the tranquillity of the Vaudois was restored, and remained undisturbed till 1571. In that year, a new and sanguinary edict was issued against them; but through the interposition of the same mediators, its fury was for a little longer averted.

New attempts were subsequently made by the Papists again to turn the valleys of Piedmont into a field of blood. The diabolical massacre of the Protestants in France on St. Bartholomew day 1572, the death of their protector the Duchess in 1574, and that of the Duke in 1580, were all seized as apparently favourable opportunities for satiating their thirst for blood in the slaughter of the Vaudois. Divine Providence, however, raised up for them friends in various quarters, through whose intercession the heart of their sovereign was touched with compassion, and the expectation of their enemies disappointed. Charles Emanuel, who succeeded his father, being importuned by the monks and priests to destroy his Waldensian subjects, the Vaudois commissioned their deputies to wait upon their prince, in order to supplicate a continuance of his favour and protection. Already made acquainted with their condition by several Protestant princes, the answer which the Duke returned, in presence of a large assembly of his lords and courtiers, was of the utmost importance to the prosperity of all the churches in Piedmont. "Be but faithful to me," said he, "and I shall not fail to be a good prince, nay, a father to you. And as to your liberty of conscience, and the exercise of your religion, I shall be so far from making any innovations in those liberties which you have enjoyed till the present time, that if any offer to molest you, have your recourse to me, and I shall effectually relieve and protect you."

The season of repose which was thus afforded to the Waldenses was seized as a favourable opportunity for holding a general assembly of the heads of families. At this meeting six articles were drawn up, which were called "the Articles of the Union of Valleys;" the object of which was to bind themselves by still more solemn ties to persevere in their religious faith, to continue to give obedience to their prince when his orders were not contrary to their conscience, and to render each other assistance in times of persecution.

These times, alas! were not far distant. About the year 1601, the inhabitants of the valley of Lucerna were so severely perse-

cuted, that many of them were obliged to
conceal their principles, and attend upon the
worship of God in private. It was in the
province of Saluzzo, or Marquisate of Saluces, however, then under the dominion of
the duke of Savoy, that the Vaudois experienced the greatest cruelties.   This province
lies on the south side of Piedmont, and is
separated from the valley of Lucerna only by
a mountain.   It is a rich tract of country,
containing several large cities, and at the
close of the sixteenth century there were
eight flourishing churches within the Marquisate.   Its contiguity to the valleys of Piedmont had frequently exposed its inhabitants
to severe sufferings; but it was not till the
year 1601 that the Romish church found an
opportunity of effecting their ruin.   In 1597,
Charles Emanuel had addressed a letter to
the churches of the Marquisate, requiring
them to " lay aside all heretical obstinacy,"
and to embrace the Roman catholic faith.
The answer which they returned, earnestly
entreated the Duke to indulge them with a
continuance of their privileges; but had not
that prince been then obliged to repair to
France, the entreaties of the Waldenses
would have been of no avail.

   In 1601, accordingly, Charles Emanuel
published an edict, " commanding all the inhabitants of the Marquisate of Saluces who

dissented from the Romish church, to appear before the magistrates within the space of fifteen days, and there declare whether they would renounce their religion, or quit the country." If the latter alternative were chosen, two months only were allowed them for leaving their homes, never to return, on pain of death. So astonished were the Waldenses at this rigorous decree, that they could not be persuaded of their sovereign being in earnest; and instead, therefore, of rendering immediate obedience to an order so unjust, they appointed deputies to wait upon the Duke, in order, if possible, to obtain some mitigation of its terms. All their efforts, however, proved abortive; and the consequence was, that five hundred families were forced to abandon all their property, and retire, some to France, and others to Geneva, or to the valleys of Piedmont. Thus were all the Vaudois churches in the Marquisate of Saluces completely dispersed.

This base action was followed, in 1602, by an edict, in which it was commanded by the Duke, "That the Vaudois should not perform any religious act beyond the limits of the valleys of Lucerna, Perosa, and San Martino, on pain of death,—that they should maintain there neither public nor private schools,—that no marriage should take place between those of different communions,—

that no Roman catholics should assist at the
Vaudois worship,—that no Vaudois should
dissuade others from attending mass, or reply
to the missionaries sent for their conversion,—
that all Vaudois should be incapable of holding any public employment whatever,—and
that no catholic, under pain of confiscation,
should sell or hire to a Vaudois either goods
or land."

In consequence of this decree, the Waldenses were exposed, till the year 1637, to innumerable vexations, and often to cruel persecution. From that period till 1650, they
enjoyed a season of tranquillity, which was
again broken in the year last mentioned by
the establishment of a council at Turin, for
the purpose of propagating the Romish faith,
and extirpating heresy. This infamous tribunal sent spies into the valleys, who attacked
the Vaudois pastors, carried off the women
and children, and cited multitudes of the inhabitants to appear before their Popish judges
at Turin, whence they were seldom allowed
to return.

The see of Rome could not, however, remain satisfied with this comparatively slow
method of accomplishing the destruction of
the Waldenses; and means more effectual,
therefore, were resorted to for effecting so
diabolical a purpose.

CHAPTER VII.

On the 25th of January 1655, the following iniquitous edict was issued by Gastaldo against the Waldenses—an edict which was executed, as the sequel will show, to its very letter:—

" We, by virtue of the authority which we hold of his royal highness, of the 13th instant, &c. command and enjoin every head of a family, with its members, of the pretended reformed religion, of what rank, degree, or condition soever, none excepted, inhabiting and possessing estates in the places of Lucerna, Lucernetta, S. Giovanni, La Torre, Bubbiana, and Fenile, Campiglione, Bricherassio, and S. Secondo, within three days after the publication of these presents, to withdraw and depart, and to be with their families withdrawn out of the said places, and transported into the places and limits tolerated by his royal highness, during his good pleasure—*under pain of death, and confiscation of houses and goods.* Provided always they do not make it appear to us within twenty days following, that they are become catholics, or that they have sold their goods to the catholics."

To comply with the terms of this decree, was to occasion inexpressible misery to the poor Waldenses. The middle of winter was the season chosen by their enemies for putting thousands of families, including the aged, the infirm, the helpless, and the sick, to flight over the rugged Alpine mountains, in traversing which it was easy to foresee that multitudes must perish. In vain, however, did they expostulate by their deputies, in the most heart-rending terms, against the cruelty of this edict. In vain did they supplicate the Duke for some mitigation of its terms. They were forced to abandon their habitations and their property, and to retire with their wives and children, conducting the halt, the lame, and the blind, and carrying the helpless infants, through a mountainous country, amidst rain, snow, and ice.

All this, however, was but the commencement of their sufferings. No sooner had they departed, than numerous lawless bands, under the sanction of Gastaldo, entered their houses, which they not only spoiled, but razed to the ground, and rendered the places adjacent a desolate wilderness. The popish army next pursued the fugitives, or attacked those who imagined they were not within the limits of the places proscribed, when scenes of perfidy, injustice, villany, and cruelty, were exhibited, which, were it not for the credibility of the numerous historians by whom they are recorded, almost exceed belief. The following mournful letter, which was written by some of the survivors of these dreadful persecutions, to their brethren in other countries, will give the reader an idea, though a very faint one, of the miseries to which the faithful and humble Waldenses were subjected.

"Brethren and Fathers!

"Our tears are no more tears of water, but of blood, which not only obscure our sight, but oppress our very hearts. Our pen is guided by a trembling hand, and our minds are distracted by such unexpected alarms, that we are incapable of forming a letter which shall correspond with our wishes, or the strangeness of our desolations. In this respect, therefore, we plead your excuse, and that you would endeavour to collect our meaning from what we would impart to you.

"Whatever reports may have been circulated, concerning our obstinacy in refusing to have recourse to his royal highness for redress of our heavy grievances and molestations, you cannot but know that we never desisted from writing supplicatory letters, or presenting our humble requests, by the hands of our deputies, and that they were sent and referred, sometimes to the council for extirpating heresies, at other times to the Marquis of Pionessa; and that the three last times they were positively rejected, and refused so much as an audience, under the pretext that they had no credentials nor instructions which should authorise them to promise or accept, on the behalf of their respective churches, whatever it might please his highness to grant or bestow upon them. And by the instigation and contrivance of the Roman clergy, there was secretly placed in ambush an army of six thousand men, who, animated and encouraged thereto by the personal presence and active exertions of the Marquis of Pionessa, fell suddenly, and in the most violent manner, upon the inhabitants of San Giovanni and La Torre.

" This army having once entered and got a footing, was soon augmented by the addition of a multitude of the neighbouring inhabitants of Piedmont, who, hearing that we were given up as a prey to the plunderers, fell upon the poor people with impetuous fury. To all those were added an incalculable number of persons that had been outlawed, prisoners, and other offenders, who expected thereby to have saved their souls, and filled their purses. And the better to effect their purposes, the inhabitants were compelled to receive five or six regiments of the French army, besides some Irish, to whom, it is reported, our country was promised, with several troops of vagabond persons, under the pretext of coming into the valleys for fresh quarters.

" This great multitude, by virtue of a license from the Marquis of Pionessa, instigated by the monks, and enticed and conducted by our wicked and unnatural neighbours, attacked us with such violence on every side, especially in Angrogna, Villaro, and Bobio, and in a manner so horribly treacherous, that in an instant all was one entire scene of confusion, and the inhabitants, after a fruitless skirmish to defend themselves, were compelled to flee for their lives, with their wives and children; and that not merely the inhabitants of the plain, but those of the mountains also. Nor was all their diligence sufficient to prevent the destruction of a considerable number of them. For, in many places, such as Villaro and Bobio, they were so hemmed in on every side, the army having seized on the fort of Mareburg, and by that means blocked up the avenue, that there remained no possibility of escape, and nothing remained to them but to be massacred and put to death. In one place they mercilessly tortured not less than a hundred and fifty women and their children, chopping off the heads of some, and dashing the brains of others against the rocks. And in regard to those whom they took prisoners, from fifteen years old and upwards, who refused to go to mass, they hanged some, and nailed others to trees by the feet, with their heads downwards. It is reported that they carried some persons of note prisoners to Turin, viz. our poor brother and pastor, Mr.

Gros, with some part of his family. In short, there are neither cattle nor provisions of any kind left in the valley of Lucerna;—it is but too evident that all is lost, since there are some whole districts, especially S. Giovanni and La Torre, where the business of setting fire to our houses and churches was so dexterously managed, by a Franciscan friar, and a certain priest, that they left not so much as one of either unburnt. In these desolations, the mother has been bereft of her dear child, the husband of his affectionate wife! Those who were once the richest amongst us, are reduced to the necessity of begging their bread; while others still remain weltering in their own blood, and deprived of all the comforts of life. And as to the churches in S. Martino and other places, who, on all former occasions, have been a sanctuary to the persecuted, they have themselves now been summoned to quit their dwellings, and every soul of them to depart, and that instantaneously and without respite, under pain of being put to death. Nor is there any mercy to be expected by any of them who are found within the dominions of his royal highness.

"The pretext which is alleged for justifying these horrid proceedings, is, that we are rebels against the orders of his highness, for not having brought the whole city of Geneva within the walls of Mary Magdalene church;

or, in plainer terms, for not having performed
an utter impossibility, in departing in a moment from our houses and homes in Bubbiana, Lucerne, Fenile, Bricheras, La Torre,
S. Giovanni, and S. Secundo; and also for
having renewed our repeated supplications
to his royal highness, to commiserate our
situation, who, while, on the one hand, he
promised us to make no innovations in our
lot, on the other refused us permission to
depart peaceably out of his dominions, which
we have often entreated him for, in case he
would not allow us to continue and enjoy the
liberty of our consciences, as his predecessors
had always done. True it is, that the marquis
of Pionessa had adduced another reason, and
we have the original copy of his writing in our
possession, which is, that it was his royal
highness's pleasure to abase us and humble
our pride, for endeavouring to shroud ourselves, and take sanctuary under the protection of foreign princes and states.

" To conclude, our beautiful and flourishing churches are utterly lost, and that without remedy, unless our God work miracles
for us. Their time is come, and our measure
is full! O have pity upon the desolations of
Jerusalem, and be grieved for the afflictions
of Joseph! Show forth your compassions, and
let your bowels yearn in behalf of so many
thousands of poor souls, who are reduced to

a morsel of bread, for following the Lamb whithersoever he goeth. We recommend our pastors, with their scattered and dispersed flocks, to your fervent christian prayers, and rest in haste,

"Your brethren in the Lord."

"*April 27th, 1655.*"

The pen almost drops from one's hand, at the touching strain of this most afflicting letter; yet it records nothing in comparison to the deeds of cruelty which are given by Morland, Leger, and other historians of equal veracity. These two writers, in particular, have embellished their works with plates, representing the tortures that were inflicted on the Vaudois, at the sight of which, the very blood freezes in the veins. To use the words of the apostle, it was literally true, that " they were stoned, they were sawn asunder, were tempted, were slain with the sword; they wandered about in sheep skins and goat skins; being destitute, afflicted, tormented, (of whom the world was not worthy;) they wandered in deserts and in mountains, and in dens and caves of the earth. "

To give any thing like an outline of the atrocities which the Papists, or rather demons in human form, committed on the servants of the Most High, would render the book in which they are stated, a horror to every virtuous and feeling mind.

The enemy, after gaining entire possession of the valleys, pretended to have no intention of remaining there more than a few days, and exhorted the Vaudois to recal their fugitive brethren, which some had the weakness to do, trusting to the assurance given them, that no harm should befal them.

"Such was the situation of affairs, when on the 24th of April, the signal was given from a hill near La Tour, called Castellas, for a general massacre, which extended through the whole valley, and began at the same instant. Neither age nor sex was spared; every refinement of cruelty which the malice of demons could invent, was put in practice. The very mention of these horrors excites too much disgust to allow of a detail of them. Violation, mutilation, and impalement, were mere common atrocities; many were roasted by slow fires, others cut in pieces while alive, or dragged by mules, with ropes passed through their wounds; some were blown up by gunpowder placed in the ears and mouth; many rolled off the rocks, with their hands bound between their legs, among precipices where they were abandoned to a cruel and lingering death; children were carried on pikes.——

"But let us not dwell longer on these infernal barbarities. They are detailed in Leger, and the names of many of the sufferers, and the evidence of eye-witnesses, are there recorded. The number who perished *in the Val Luzerne alone*, amounted to two hundred and fifty, besides children and others, whose names have not been collected, and the men, who fell sword in hand: for nearly all the victims of these cruelties were women, children, and old people. But the mere recital of the numbers destroyed, cannot suffice to give an idea of the miseries endured; we must add the horrors encountered by the survivors, wandering in utter destitution among the mountains, in terror and want, after witnessing the murder and outrages committed on their dearest relatives and friends."*

The report of this inhuman massacre raised in every Protestant state of Europe, as we shall afterwards see, a universal feeling of horror. The chief agents in these deeds of blood found it necessary, therefore, to endeavour to extenuate their enormities, and every

* The Marquis of Piannezza was so enraged at the escape of Gianavello, who with a handful of men had nobly defended the village of Roia and thrice repulsed the murderous assailants, although thousands in number, that he threatened to torture his wife and children, whom he had taken prisoners, unless he surrendered himself and changed his religion. Gianavello, however, returned the Marquis the following noble answer:—" No torture is so horrible, nor is any death so cruel, which I would not prefer to the abjuration of my faith, which the threats of the Marquis only serve to confirm. As to my wife and children, whom he has in his power, Providence will not abandon them. If he is permitted to put them to death, he can do no more than kill their bodies. As to their souls, which will accuse him before the throne of the God of the universe, I commend them and my own to the Divine protection."

one attempted to throw the odium upon his fellow.

The news of the dreadful sufferings to which the Waldenses were subjected, no sooner reached the Protestant states of Europe, than a sensation was felt, which perhaps was never expressed for a similar cause, in a manner so decided and universal. The English government, the kings of France, Sweden, and Denmark, the Swiss Cantons, the States General of the United Provinces, the Duke of Wirtemberg, the Elector Palatine, the Elector of Brandenburg, the Landgrave of Hesse, and the Republic of Geneva, all interested themselves in the afflictions of the Waldenses. Letters were written, and envoys dispatched, from these powers to the Duke of Savoy, interceding for the persecuted Vaudois, and remonstrating against the injustice and barbarity of their oppressors. The Swiss cantons, in particular, who were the first to hear of these horrid massacres, not only wrote to the Duke, but set apart a day for public humiliation, fasting, and prayer, and recommended a general collection to be made throughout all their territories for the relief of the sufferers.

But among all the powers who interested themselves in behalf of the poor Vaudois, none took a more decided part than that of England. Urged on by the poet Milton, who at that time filled the office of Latin Secretary, Oliver Cromwell immediately wrote, not only to the Duke of Savoy, but to all the Pro·testant princes and states in Europe, entreating their aid in vindicating and relieving the sufferers. Milton, indeed, was so deeply affected at the account of their miseries, which was transmitted to .England, that it drew from his pen the following touching sonnet:—

"Avenge, O Lord, thy slaughtered saints, whose
    bones
Lie scattered on the Alpine mountains cold:
Even them, who kept thy truth so pure of old,
When all our fathers worshipped stocks and stones,
Forget not; in thy book record their groans
Who were thy sheep, and in their ancient fold
Slain by the bloody Piedmontese, that roll'd
Mother with infant down the rocks. Their moans
The vales redoubled to the hills, and they
To Heaven. Their martyr'd blood and ashes sow
O'er all the Italian fields where still doth sway
The triple tyrant; that from these may grow
An hundred fold, who, having learnt thy way,
Early may fly the Babylonian woe."

The following is the letter which Cromwell the Protector addressed to the Duke of Savoy.

"Most Serene Prince,

"We have received letters from several places in the vicinity of your dominions, informing us that the subjects of your royal highness, professing the Reformed religion, have been commanded by an edict, published by your authority, under pain of death and the confiscation of their property, to quit their houses and lands, unless they shall enter into an engagement to abjure their own religion, and embrace the Roman Catholic faith, before the end of twenty days. And we have also learnt, that, regardless of their humble petitions to your royal highness, praying for a revocation of that edict, and to grant them the same privileges which were granted them by your serene predecessors, your army fell upon them, cruelly massacred great numbers, imprisoned others, and drove the rest into desolate places and to mountains covered with snow, where hundreds of families are reduced to such extremity, that it is to be feared they will all soon perish with cold and hunger.

"On receiving intelligence of the awful condition of this most miserable people, it was impossible not to feel the deepest sorrow and compassion; for, we not only consider ourselves united to them by the ties of humanity, but those of the same religion. Feeling, therefore, that we should fail in our duty to God, to our brethren, to ourselves, and to the religion we profess, and should evince the want of brotherly love, if we were not deeply moved by a sense of their calamities, we declare that we feel it necessary to use every means in our power to obtain an alleviation of their unparalleled sufferings.

" We therefore most earnestly entreat and
conjure your highness, in the first place, to
call to mind the acts and ordinances of your
ancestors, and the concessions which they
made and confirmed from time immemorial
in favour of their subjects in the valleys:
which concessions were granted unquestion-
ably in obedience to the will of God, who re-
quires that liberty of conscience should be
the inviolable right of every man, and in
consideration of the merits of these their subjects, whom they always found faithful in
war, and obedient in time of peace. And as
your highness has imitated the example of
your ancestors in all other things that have
been so gloriously achieved by them, we again
and again beseech you, that you will not depart from them in this instance, but that you
will revoke this edict, and any other that has
been issued for the disquieting of your subjects on account of their religion; that you
will restore to them their houses and property; that you will confirm to them their ancient
rights and liberties; that you will cause re-
paration to be made for the injuries they have
sustained; and adopt such means as may put
an end to these vexatious proceedings. In
doing this, your highness will perform what
is most acceptable to God, comfort and support the minds of these unhappy sufferers,
and give satisfaction to all your neighbours

who profess the Protestant religion, especially to us, who will regard your clemency as
the effect of our intercession; which will con-
strain us to do every kind office in return,
and will be the means of not only renewing
our good correspondence and friendship, but
of increasing them between this commonwealth and your dominions. Promising ourselves much from your justice and clemency,
we earnestly pray to God to incline your
mind and thoughts, and so to confer on you
and on your people the blessings of peace and
truth, and to prosper you in all your affairs.
    "Given at our Court, at Westminister,
       May 25, 1655.
                        "Oliver, Protector."
    Cromwell next ordered a general fast, and
had a narrative printed and circulated through
the country, representing the miseries of the
Waldenses, and recommending a general con-
tribution. As an example of the liberality
which he wished to see manifested by the nation, he contributed, from his own private
purse, the sum of two thousand pounds ster-
ling, (about 8900 dollars;) and a sum was
soon raised, which amounted to £38,241,
(about 179,960 dollars.) He likewise wrote
to the Kings of France, Denmark, and Sweden,
and to the States General of the United Provinces, calling upon them to join with himself
in endeavouring to relieve the wants, and

secure the safety and liberty of the unhappy sufferers.

He appointed Sir Samuel Morland immediately to repair to Turin, to present letters of strong remonstrance to the Duke, and to express the indignation which the proceedings against the Waldenses had excited in Britain. Morland arrived at Rivoli, within two miles of Turin, on the 21st of June. He obtained an audience on the 23d, when in presence of the Duke, Madame Royale, and the whole court, he delivered an oration in which he displayed so much ardour, faithfulness, and judgment, that it will not be thought unnecessary to give it here.

" May it please your most serene and royal highness,

" I am sent by the most serene prince Oliver, lord protector of the commonwealth of England, Scotland, and Ireland, unto your royal highness, whom he heartily saluteth.— Though I be a young man, and have not much experience in affairs, yet it pleased my master to send me to your royal highness, to negotiate matters of great importance, for so those affairs are to be called, wherein the safety of many poor distressed people, and also all their hope, are comprehended, which, indeed, consisteth wholly in this, if so be that by all their loyalty, obedience, and most humble petitions, they may be able to mollify and ap pease the mind of your royal highness, which hath been provoked against them.

" In behalf of these poor people, whose cause, truly, even commiseration itself may seem to make the more excusable, the protector of England is also become an intercessor; and he most earnestly entreateth and beseecheth your royal highness, that you would be pleased to extend your mercy to these your very poor subjects, and most disconsolate outcasts: I mean those who, inhabiting beneath the Alps, and certain valleys under your dominions, are professors of the Protestant religion. For he hath been informed, that part of these most miserable people have been cruelly massacred by your forces, part driven out by violence, and forced to leave their native habitations; and so, without house or shelter, poor, and destitute of all relief, do wander up and down, with their wives and children, in craggy and uninhabitable places, and mountains covered with snow. Oh! the fired houses which are yet smoking, the torn limbs, and ground defiled with blood!—

" Men, an hundred years old, decrepit with age and bedrid, have been burnt in their beds. Infants have been dashed against the rocks, have had their throats cut, and their brains, with more than Cyclopean cruelty, have been boiled and eaten by the murderers!! What

need I mention more, although I could reckon
up very many cruelties of the same kind, if
I were not astonished at the very thought of
them. If all the tyrants of all times and
places were alive again, certainly they would
be ashamed when they should find, that they
had contrived nothing in comparison with
these things that might be reputed barbarous
and inhuman.

"The very angels are surprised with horror at them! Men are amazed! Heaven itself
seems to be astonished with the cries of dying
men; and the very earth to blush, being dis-
coloured with the gore of so many innocent
persons! Do not thou, O thou most high
God, do not thou take that revenge which is
due to so great wickedness and horrible vil-
lanies! Let thy blood, O Christ, wash away
this blood!

"But it is not my business to make a narrative of these things, in order as they were
done, or to insist any longer upon them; and
that which my most serene master desireth
of your royal highness, you will better understand by his own letters, which letters I am
commanded, with all observance and due respect, to deliver unto your royal highness; to
which if your royal highness shall, as we
very much hope, be pleased to vouchsafe a
speedy answer, you will thereby very highly
oblige my lord Protector, who hath laid this

thing deeply to heart, and the whole commonwealth of England. You will also, by an
act of compassion most worthy of your royal
highness, restore life, safety, and spirit, country and estates, to many thousands of afflicted
people, who depend upon your pleasure; and
you will dismiss me back to my native country with exceeding joy, and with a report of
your eminent virtues, the most happy pro-
claimer of your princely clemency, and one
for ever most obliged to your royal highness."

No sooner had Morland concluded his
speech, than Madame Royale addressed herself to the English minister, and informed
him, "that as, on the one hand, she could
not but extremely applaud the singular charity
and goodness of his highness, the lord protector, towards their subjects, whose situation
had been represented to him so exceedingly
lamentable, as she perceived by his discourse
had been done, so, on the other, she could
not but extremely wonder that the malice of
men should ever proceed so far as to clothe
such *paternal and tender chastisements* of
their *most rebellious* and *insolent* subjects, in
characters so black and deformed, thereby to
render them odious to all the neighbouring
princes and states, with whom they were so
anxious to keep up a good understanding and
friendship, especially with so great and power

ful a prince as the lord protector. But she was persuaded, when he came to be more particularly informed of the truth of all that had passed, he would be so perfectly satisfied with the Duke's proceedings, that he would not give the least countenance to his *disobedient subjects.* However, for his highness's sake, they would not only freely pardon their rebellious subjects for the *very heinous crimes* which they had committed, but would also grant them such privileges and favours, as could not fail to give the protector full proof of the great respect which they entertained for his person and mediation."

The result was, that the Duke of Savoy returned an answer to Cromwell, promising to proclaim a general act of indemnity, to restore the Vaudois to their possessions, and to concede the same privileges and immunities which his ancestors had granted; and he concluded by referring all differences to the mediation of the king of France. England and the rest of the Protestant powers were completely thrown off their guard by these promises; the courts of France and Savoy took advantage of the satisfaction which was expressed at the matter having been left to be so arranged, and huddled up a treaty, called the Treaty of Pignerol, which left the poor Vaudois at the mercy of their oppressors,

under the mask of establishing their security."

That this treaty gave no security, the poor
Waldenses soon felt by sad experience. They
therefore drew up on the 29th March 1656,
a pathetic appeal for redress, entitled, " The
Grievances of the Treaty made at Pignerol,"
which, though a most affecting document, our
limits prevent us from laying before the reader.   It was delivered to the king of France;
but no redress could be obtained.   " It so
happened," says Morland, " that from this
time forward, the leading men in the court
of Savoy have used their best endeavours to
lay heavier loads on their backs than ever
they had hitherto done.   For in their orders
of 20th April and 6th October 1656, and
24th August 1657, they summoned the poor
people to pay their taxes for the year 1655,
contrary to the treaty, while they exempted
the Catholics from the said taxes : and when
they appealed to the Duke, 6th October 1657,
on the hardship of their case, they were,
among other things, absolutely prohibited the
exercise of their public worship in San Giovanni."

Having remained among the Waldenses
till the summer of 1658, Morland closes his
nistory in the following mournful words:—
'It is my unhappiness that I am forced to

leave them where I found them, among the potsherds, with sackcloth and ashes spread under them, and lifting up their voice with weeping, in the words of Job, ' Have pity on us, have pity on us, O ye our friends, for the hand of God hath touched us.' To this very hour they hunger and thirst, and are naked and buffetted, and have no certain dwelling-place. To this very day they labour under most heavy burdens, which are laid upon them by their rigid task-masters of the church of Rome; by forbidding them all manner of traffic or commerce for their sustenance, by robbing them of their goods and estates, by banishing their ministers, who are the shepherds of the flocks, that so the wolves may the better devour the sheep; yea, by murdering many innocents as they pass along the high-way; by cruel mockings and revilings; by continual menacings and threats of another massacre, if possible sevenfold more bloody than the former!—To all which I must add, that notwithstanding those supplies which have been sent them from England and other states, yet so great is the number of those hungry creatures, and so grievous are the oppressions of their popish enemies, who lie. in wait to bereave them of whatsoever is given them, and snatch at every morsel of meat that goes into their mouths, that to this day they are ready to eat their own flesh for want of bread. The tongue of the suckling is ready to cleave to the roof of his mouth, and the young children ask bread, and no man gives it to them; and in many places the young and the old lie on the ground in the streets. Their miseries are more grievous than words can express. They have ' no grapes in their vineyards; no cattle in their fields; no herds in their stalls; no corn in their garners; no meal in their barrels; no oil in their cruse.' The stock which was gathered for them by the good people of this and other nations, is wasting apace, and when that is spent, they must inevitably perish, except God, who turns the hearts of princes as the rivers of water, be graciously pleased to incline the heart of their sovereign prince, to take pity on his poor, harmless, and faithful subjects."

The flames of persecution were not however confined to Piedmont. Similar deeds of cruelty were inflicted on the Waldenses of Poland, a full account of which was published at the time, (1658,) in England, and again excited the sympathy and liberality of the British nation. But the details of this horrid work presents a picture of human depravity too gross for our readers.

CHAPTER VIII.

NOTWITHSTANDING the disadvantageous terms of the treaty of Pignerol, numbers of the Waldenses who had fled from the massacres of 1665, returned to their native valleys. But, alas! it was only to endure still farther persecutions, and to share with their brethren the sufferings to which the Romish church subjected all who dared to call in question her usurped and despotic power. To this state of continual affliction the Waldenses patiently submitted till 1672, when Providence gave them an opportunity of signalizing their loyalty to their prince, which, for some time, procured for them a considerable portion of tranquillity.

A war having broken out in 1672, between the duke of Savoy and the Genoese, in which the latter proved almost uniformly victorious, the Waldenses, notwithstanding their former ill treatment, voluntarily came forward to the assistance of their sovereign. This reinforcement to the duke's army, gave a new turn to the contest, which shortly afterwards ended in the complete discomfiture of the Genoese. In testimony of gratitude for their loyalty on this occasion, the duke addressed to the Waldenses the following letter, acknowledging the obligations under which he was laid for their services, and promising them his favour and protection.

"To our most faithful subjects, the communities of the valleys of Lucerna, Perouse, S. Martino, and of the districts of Perrus tin, &c. &c.

"*The Duke of Savoy, Prince of Piedmont, &c.*

"MOST DEAR AND FAITHFUL,

"Forasmuch as we have been well pleased with the zeal and readiness with which you have provided men, who have served us to our entire satisfaction, in the affair we had against the Genoese,—we have thought fit to testify unto you by these presents, our approbation thereof, and to assure you, that we shall keep it in particular remembrance, to make you sensible on all occasions of the effects of our royal protection, whereof the count Beccaria shall give you more ample information, whom we have commanded to express to you our sentiments more at large, and also to take a list of the officers and soldiers, as well of those that are dead, as of those that remain prisoners, that he may report the same unto us, to the end that we may pay regard thereunto. In the meantime, these presents shall serve you for an assured testi-

mony of our satisfaction and good will; and
we pray God to preserve you from evil.

(Signed) "C. EMANUEL.

"*Turin, 5th Nov.* 1672."

Nor were these mere words of course; for
till the period of his death, which took place
in 1675, he continued to be their steady
friend. Following his example, the Duchess
extended to the Vaudois the same sympathy
and kindness; and till the year 1685, the
Waldensian churches "had rest throughout
all Piedmont; and, walking in the fear of the
Lord, and in the comfort of the Holy Ghost,
were multiplied."

But this season of tranquillity was very
short lived. New scenes of violence and injustice were acted in the devoted valleys of
Piedmont; and, to use the words of the pro-
phet, "destruction upon destruction was
cried; for the whole land was spoiled." Victor Amadeus II. was now the sovereign of the
Vaudois; and, though numerous proclamations
had been issued, one of them even so late as
in 1684, all acknowledging their inviolable
attachment to their princes, yet that unfeeling
potentate published an edict in January 1686,
ordering "that every Protestant church and
chapel should be razed to the ground, and that
every person professing the Protestant faith,
should publicly renounce his errors, within

fifteen days from the date of the proclamation,
under pain of banishment or death.   All infants, too, born from that time, were to be
brought up in the Roman Catholic religion,
under the penalty of their fathers being condemned to the gallies!"

In vain did the Waldenses themselves, or
the Protestant states of Europe, remonstrate
against so unjust an edict. Amidst tears and
expostulations, the duke, urged on by the
king of France, proceeded to put his dreadful
decree into execution.   The Waldenses had
now, therefore, no other alternative but to
arm in their own defence; and though out of
a population of about 15,000, only 2500 were
capable of bearing arms, yet this handful
more than once repulsed the united forces of
the king of France, and the duke of Savoy.
"The Vaudois," says Gilly, "gallantly withstood the first shock of war, and for three
days, were victorious in every engagement.
At length they were compelled, by the over-
whelming numbers of their invaders, to submit, but not before such horrible devastation
had been carried into every hamlet, and such
unheard of barbarities committed upon all
ages, even upon women and infants, that it
would be outraging human nature to recount
them." More than three thousand are said to
have prerished either by the sword, or by the
more horrible inventions of their persecutors;

ten thousand were imprisoned or banished,
and multitudes of children were conducted to
remote places, to be educated in the Popish
faith. "The jails," says Boyer, "were so
full of these wretched people, that they perished by hundreds, of hunger, thirst, and
infectious diseases. It would be a hard matter
to represent all the miseries and calamities
they suffered during their captivity; and they
were more or less ill treated according to the
ill humour of those who had the command of
their prisons. They had nothing but bread
and water for their ordinary food; the one
without substance, and the other from the
kennels of the streets. In some places they
gave them water only at certain set times, and
in such small quantities, that many perished.
They slept on the bare bricks; or, if they
were allowed straw, it was rotten, and full of
vermin, while the dungeons were so thronged,
that they were crowded to suffocation. The
place of the dead, numbers of them dying
every day, was constantly supplied with fresh
prisoners, that the dungeons might be always
equally thronged; and the intense heat of the
summer, and the corruption with which the
chambers were infected, by reason of the
great number of the sick, engendered evils
too horrible for recital."

At the end of six months, three thousand
only, of the prisoners remained alive, and

even of these it may be said, that they were
little more than the shadows of human beings.
For this miserable remnant, however, the protestant states again made so urgent intercess-
sion, that Victor Amadeus, in the middle of
winter, issued a proclamation for releasing
them, on condition of their banishing themselves for ever from Piedmont. "The pro
clamation," says Jones, "was made at the
castle of Mondovi, for example, and at five
o'clock *the same evening* they were to begin
a march of four or five leagues; before the
morning, more than a hundred and fifty of
them sunk under the burden of their maladies
and fatigue, and died. The same thing happened to the prisoners at Fossan. A company of them halted one night at the foot of
Mount Cenis; when they were about to march
the next morning, they pointed the officer
who conducted them, to a terrible tempest
upon the top of the mountain, beseeching him
to allow them to stay till it had passed away.
The inhuman officer, deaf to the voice of pity,
insisted on their marching; the consequence
of which was, that eighty-six of their number
died, and were buried in that horrible tempest of snow. Some merchants that afterwards
crossed the mountains, saw the bodies of these
miserable people extended on the snow, the
mothers clasping the children in their arms!
Such as survived, reached Geneva about the

end of December, but in such an exhausted
state, that many of them died upon their
arrival, 'finding the end of their life in the
beginning of their liberty.' Of about ten
thousand that were imprisoned in Piedmont,
not more than a fourth part survived, but
these were received by the citizens of Geneva,
and also in Switzerland, with more kindness
than they had experienced of cruelty from the
Piedmontese. Thus were the valleys of Piedmont dispeopled of their ancient inhabitants,
and the lamp of heavenly light, which, during
a long sucession of ages, had here shined in
resplendent lustre, was at length removed."

Having thus triumphed over the faithful
Vaudois, and expelled them from their native
valleys, the pefidious Victor Amadeus II. re-
peopled Piedmont with Roman Catholics,
and placed garrisons of French and Piedmontese soldiers in the forts which guarded
the passes of the mountains. The ancient
inhabitants were now scattered among different nations, and nothing seemed to be more
improbable, than that they should ever return, and take possession of that country
from which they had been so unjustly expatriated.

In vain, however, do men attempt to thwart
the purposes of the Most High; it is "his
counsel" alone that "shall stand," and
"when He works, none can let it." Raised

up by Divine Providence, Henri Arnaud,
one of the Waldensian pastors, undertook
the arduous enterprise of conducting the
scattered Vaudois to Piedmont, and of re-
settling them among their native mountains.
With that love of their native country which
distinguishes the inhabitants of these mountains, and the recollections of a church which
had maintained its purity for ages amidst
these secure retreats, they were incited by
the most powerful motives to regain possession of their own hills and valleys. The following is the account which is given us by
Gilly, of this disinterested and Christian pa-
triot.

" Ardent, enthusiastic, and patriotic, Henri
Arnaud's love for his native valleys would
not suffer him to be happy in a foreign land;
his courage would hear of no obstacles, and
his warm imagination represented the arm of
God as lifted up to succour the holy under-
taking. *The light shineth in darkness*, was
the motto of his community, and the words
which were ever in his mouth. He thought
he saw the cloud which was to go before him
by day, and the pillar of fire which was to
give him light by night, and he was incessant
in his importunities, until he had communicated his own spirit to a few faithful friends,
and had girt on his sword, which he solemn-
ly swore never to resign, until the valley

churches were free from pollution. In a
short time, his little troop was increased to
upwards of eight hundred daring adventurers,
whom he had persuaded to join his standard,
from different parts of Germany and Switzerland. They were obliged to meet in secret,
and their nocturnal assemblies were held in
the dark retreats of a forest, which then
spread over a long tract of country, between
Niou and Rolle, and extended down to the
edge of the lake of Geneva."

The preparations of Arnaud were completed on the evening of the 16th of August
1689. He had previously made two attempts
to lead his heroic band into Piedmont; but
both had failed, and additional guards were
stationed on the frontiers by the Duke of
Savoy. On the above mentioned night, however, Arnaud and his men crossed the lake
in boats which they had seized on the coast,
and landed between Nernier and Yvoire in
Savoy. Here they would have been attacked
by an armed force, had they not laid hold of
two gentlemen, whom they detained as hostages, till they were beyond the reach of danger from the inhabitants of that part of the
country. For two or three days they travel-
led through places to which they were total
strangers, and had it not been for their guides,
for whose fidelity their hostages were an-
swerable, in all probability they would have

fallen into the hands of the enemy. Their
utmost vigilance, indeed, scarcely prevented
them from being betrayed. The inhabitants
of Clauses, not only at first refused to grant
them a passage through their territories, but
despatched messengers to Sallanches, exhorting the inhabitants of that city to attack the
Vaudois in front, while they themselves would
assail them in the rear. This scheme, however, was most providentially frustrated, and
the Waldenses continued their march, not
without considerable opposition, till they arrived at Cablau, where they remained for the
night. The rain fell in torrents during the
whole of that day, which rendered their
march both difficult and hazardous; yet,
"even for this rain," says Arnaud, "these
poor people had cause to be thankful, as it
no doubt prevented the enemy from pursuing
them."

On the following morning, they ascended
the mountain Haut Luce, amidst rain, snow,
and fog; and had it not been for the intrepid-
ity of their leader, their guides would have
conducted them into places where they would
easily have become a prey to their enemies.*

* The guides "maliciously contrived," says Arnaud, "to lead the Vaudois through the most frightful passes, to allow time for the Savoyards to come
up and destroy them; and, in consequence, Mons.
Arnaud threatened to have these treacherous guides

Their exertions and fatigues were still farther increased during the fourth day's march, in the morning of which they ascended, or rather climbed, among snow above two feet deep, the mountain Bon Homme. After encountering innumerable difficulties and dangers, they at length " descended from these snow-covered heights, and followed the course of the mountain torrent called Reclus, and penetrated through a woody ravine into the plain of Scez."

It was not, however, till the eighth day of their enterprise that they first came in contact with any large disciplined army. A strong garrison of soldiers had been placed at Susa, whom the Waldenses wished if possible to avoid, and accordingly proceeded along the banks of the river Doire, till they arrived at

hanged. If the zealous leader of this little troop knew how to alarm those who meant to deceive, he endeavoured no less, by good and holy exhortations, to raise the courage of those under his care, and who seemed now on the point of sinking under an accumulation of evils, increased by the almost unbearable fatigue of effecting a passage through a pass cut in the rock, like a ladder, where twenty persons might easily have destroyed 20,000. They descended with greater difficulty; and in a sitting posture slid down precipices, without any other light than what was afforded them by the snow, and arrived late in the night at St. Nicholas de Verose, a miserable hamlet, composed merely of some shepherds' huts."

within a short distance of Salabertran, where
a bridge is thrown across the current. Here
they found a body of 2500 French soldiers
ready to oppose them, who, on their approach,
summoned them to lay down their arms, and
surrender themselves prisoners. The situation of the Vaudois at this critical juncture
was truly distressing. Worn out with fatigue, opposed by a force so very superior
in point of numbers, and unable to effect a
retreat from the nature of the place, and from
the garrison of Susa, which was ready to attack them in the rear,—they had now no alternative but to advance and endeavour to
render themselves masters of the bridge.
The conflict which followed cannot be described in better terms than in the words of
the undaunted Arnaud himself.

"An engagement now appearing to be in-
evitable, the Vaudois assembled to prayers;
and, having reconnoitred the ground on each
side, advanced almost to the bridge. Some
of the enemy, who were intrenched on the
other side, called out *who goes there?* to
which they replied very sincerely, *friends,*
that was, provided they were allowed to pass;
but the others, who desired no friends at that
price, cried, ' Kill them, kill them,' and opened upon them a fire which lasted more than a
quarter of an hour, during which more than
two thousand shots were discharged. Ar-

naud having at first ordered his men to lie
down flat on their faces, one man only was
wounded. A Savoyard nobleman, one of the
hostages, declared that he had never seen so
terrible a firing take such little effect; and
what was still more remarkable, Arnaud,
Captain Mondon, and two other refugees,
were not only obliged to expose themselves
to it, but held in check two companies who
attempted to charge the Vaudois in the rear.
Our men, seeing themselves thus placed between two fires, and that every exertion must
be made to carry the bridge, it so animated the
soldiers, that they threw themselves upon it,
and forcing it sword in hand, made their way
into the entrenchments of the enemy, whom
they pursued so closely as to seize them by
the hair. The shock was tremendous. The
sabres of the Vaudois shivered the swords of
the French in pieces, who could use their
muskets only to parry the blows. At length
the victory was so complete, that the Marquis
de Larrey, who commanded the French, and
was dangerously wounded in the arm, exclaimed, 'Is it possible that I should lose
both the battle and my honour? Save himself who can!' He then retreated with several
wounded officers to Briançon, where not
thinking himself in safety, he fled in a litter
to Embrun. The engagement lasted nearly
two hours, and the enemy were thrown into

such disorder, that many were mixed with
the Vaudois and killed. At last the field of
battle remained covered with the dead; many
companies were reduced to seven or eight men,
all their officers having been killed. All the
baggage and ammunition fell into the hands
of the victorious Vaudois, who made the air
resound with this exclamation of joy, 'Thanks
be given to the eternal God of armies, who
has granted us the victory.'

" What! could a handful of men force 2500
soldiers from their entrenchments, when of
these soldiers nineteen companies were composed of regular troops, and the remainder
of militia and peasants, besides the troops in
their rear, already mentioned ? The thing
appears so improbable, that to believe it, one
must bear firmly in mind that the hand of
God not only fought for them, but blinded the
French, otherwise it is impossible that a nation so clear-sighted, and so skilful in the
art of war, should have failed to perceive,
that by breaking up the bridge, which was
only of wood, they must have instantly stopt
the progress of the Vaudois, for the river was
so swollen, that it was not fordable. Asto-
nishing as this victory appears, the trifling
loss sustained by the victors is not less so;
from ten to twelve only were wounded, and
fourteen or fifteen killed."

This signal defeat not only raised the spi-

rits of the victors, but struck terror into the
hearts of the vanquished. Instead therefore
of taking repose, the little band of Vaudois
pressed forward and encountered and defeated
another large body of the enemy. It was in
the valley of Angrogna, however, where the
greater part of the Popish army was concen-
trated, to dislodge whom the Vaudois were
determined to make every exertion. All the
passes were fortified by the French and
Piedmontese, and the efforts of Arnaud to
effect an entrance into Angrogna seemed to
be altogether hopeless. But nothing could
check his impetuous attack. The heights
were carried with little or no loss on the part
of the Waldenses, and the Popish forces
were pursued from one summit to another,
till at length they took refuge in the village
of Bobbi. Nor were they secure even there.
The victorious Arnaud soon made himself
master of that place also, the garrison having
fled at his approach, and its spoil was distributed among the conquerors.

The successes with which the arms of the
Vaudois were crowned, never inspired them
with self-confidence. They knew upon whose
smile or frown depended the prosperity or
the failure of their enterprise; and they never
ceased therefore to implore the God of their
fathers, to be the breaker up of the way before them. On the 28th of August, they cele-

brated divine service for the first time since their banishment, in one of their own churches. Having sung the 74th Psalm, Arnaud mounted the pulpit, and preached from the 129th Psalm, and " once more declared in the face of heaven, that he would never resume his pastoral office in patience and peace, until he should witness the restoration of his brethren to their ancient and rightful settlements." They also took an oath of fidelity to each other, binding themselves " neither to separate nor disunite while granted life by God, even though they should be reduced to the number of three or four."

Unintimidated by numbers, the Vaudois next turned their arms against Villars, where there was a strong garrison, and pressed the enemy so hard, as to force them to retire within the walls of a convent. From this position they would soon have been dislodged, had not a strong reinforcement arrived from Pignerol, which obliged the Waldenses to retire to the mountains of S. Martino. Strong detachments of French and Piedmontese troops were now dispatched to all the valleys, to pursue and crush the intrepid Arnaud and his little band; and wherever these forces marched, they desolated the country, in order to cut off all supplies of provisions from the Vaudois. The warfare now assumed a more extraordinary turn than ever. The eight hundred had to maintain their ground against brigades sent against them by the King of France on the one side, and the Duke of Savoy on the other: it was no longer a detached force, but a well-appointed army, with which they had now to contend. The rocky and barren district of San Martino afforded them no resources; the defiles that led into the more fertile valleys were in the hands of the enemy; famine, fire, and sword, menaced them in every direction; and yet they refused to surrender. Even the fastnesses which in former persecutions protected their fathers, were untenable for any length of time, from want of provisions. Scarcely had they taken up a position, before they were obliged to abandon it, in search of supplies; and it is an extraordinary fact, that for several weeks they had neither food nor ammunition but such as they took from the enemy. Under these circumstances, it was impossible that the little band should concentrate its force, or remain together. It was obliged to separate, and to act in detached parties. Engagements were therefore taking place almost every day, in different quarters of the valley; the enemy never knew where they would be attacked next, and at length were so intimidated, that a whole company would fly at the sound of a single Waldensian fusil. One great thing in favour of this intrepid force

was, that they had no women or children to
encumber them, for these were still in Switzerland; there was nothing to check the freedom of their movements, and few strong places
to attack or defend, for what were strong
places to them?—As the winter set in, the
hardships and deprivations of these poor men
increased; without any shelter for several
nights together, worn down by constant
fatigue, and half famished for want of food,
it is wonderful how they supported their
courage."

Still, however, the Vaudois, under the protection of Divine Providence, kept in check
for some time longer the powerful forces with
which they were surrounded; but at length,
finding their positions to be no longer tenable,
they resolved to retire to Balsille, the only
fort which now remained in their hands.
This fort was situated at the entrance of the
pass which conducted into the valley of S.
Martino, and was so strongly fortified by nature, as well as by art, that it was deemed
quite impregnable.   The Vaudois set out
from Lucerna, on their way to Balsille, towards the end of October, by a path which
was so exceedingly difficult that the whole of
their baggage was lost.   "The road they
were obliged to take," says Arnaud, " was so
interrupted by precipices, that they were often
obliged to crawl along on their hands and

feet, and every man having enough to do to take care of himself, the hostages found means to escape. To prove how clearly Providence watched over them, two wounded men passed this road safely on horseback. Those who have never seen such kind of places cannot form any idea of the danger and difficulty attached to them; and those who have, will take this march for fiction; however, that which is here related is the simple truth. And it may be further added, that when the Vaudois afterwards saw by day-light the places they had passed by night, they shuddered at the idea of the dangers which they had escaped."

In a few days after the Waldenses had arrived at Balsille, which they rendered still stronger by their fortifications, the French and Piedmontese forces commenced their attack. Scarcely a single day passed without an engagement taking place, in which the besieged proved uniformly victorious; while, from the nature of the place, and the terror which the Vaudois arms struck into the enemy, the most dreadful slaughter was made among the forces of the besiegers. And what was still more lamentable, the Vaudois, having no means of providing for the security of the prisoners, were compelled, for their own safety, to put to the sword every man that fell into their hands. The conflict consequently was most sanguinary; and Arnaud

himself often laments the cruel necessity under which they were laid to shed the blood
of their enemies.

After eight months the fearful odds in point
of numbers, however, at length made the
Vaudois give way, and the lower part of the
fort of Balsille was carried by assault.
Nothing could now save the Waldenses but
a speedy flight; and while preparations were
making by the enemy for attacking their remaining entrenchments, Arnaud and his followers abandonod Balsille on the evening of
the 14th of May 1690. "The immense fires
kept burning in the encampment," says Arnaud, "seemed to preclude all hope of their
being able to retire under cover of the night,
and well were they aware that the hand of
God alone could deliver them in this hour of
peril, as he had already done from so many
former dangers. But at the very moment
when a most cruel death seemed to be pre-
paring for them, a fog arose before dark which
lengthened the night, it being too short at that
season of the year for their purpose. Having
accurately observed the situation of the
enemy's fires, the only chance of escape
seemed to be across a frightful precipitous
ravine. They proceeded down this chasm,
some sliding on their backs, other scrambling
with one knee on the ground, holding by the
branches of trees, and feeling their way with

their hands or feet. In this way they passed close to one of the French outposts, and ascended the mountain of Guignevert, and two hours afterwards they were still climbing the mountain by steps which they had cut for themselves in the snow."

When the enemy entered the fort, and found not one Vaudois on whom to wreak their vengeance, their mortification was extreme.* Detachments were sent out in every direction to pursue the fugitives, who were hunted from one mountain to another, and exposed to privations and sufferings the most severe. Still, however, the Vaudois scorned to yield; and from their intimate knowledge of the numerous fastnesses with which they were surrounded, and the expertness which they displayed in seizing every opportunity which offered to attack their enemies, the Popish troops found it no easy matter to surprise, far less to subdue them.

While the contest remained in this uncertain, and, in regard to the Vaudois, danger-

* "The disappointment of the French," says Arnaud, "was embittered by the fact, that the day before the attack, they had proclaimed with the sound of the trumpet, that all who wished to witness the end of the Vaudois should come to Pignerol on the morrow, where the Vaudois would be hung two and two: but, alas! the promised spectacle was changed for the mortifying one of the arrival of many waggons full of their own wounded."

ous condition, He who " will not suffer his people to be tried above what they are able to bear," brought it at length to a happy termination. The King of France and the Duke of Savoy having quarrelled between themselves, the arms of these persecutors were turned against each other. Aware of the bravery of Arnaud and his little troop, and desirous of securing their services in his conflict with the French monarch, the Duke of Savoy offered them terms of peace exceedingly favourable. Ever loyal to their legitimate sovereign, notwithstanding all his ingratitude, the Waldenses joyfully acceded to his proposals. A treaty was soon signed, and a general amnesty proclaimed by the Duke, in which the exiles were permitted to return to their native valleys, their churches re-opened, and their houses and lands restored. When the Vaudois prisoners throughout Piedmont were released, the Duke of Savoy addressed them in the words following:—"You have but one God and one prince to serve: serve God and your prince faithfully. Till now we have been enemies, henceforth we must be good friends; others have been the cause of your misfortune, (meaning the King of France,) but if now, as you ought, you expose your lives for my service, I will expose mine also for yours; and while I have a morsel of bread, you shall have your share."

Thus were the Waldenses once more settled in peace among their native mountains; in effecting which the hand of a superintending and all-wise Providence must be apparent to every reflecting mind. The following are the reflections of Arnaud upon this interesting and surprising event, which cannot fail to be read with the liveliest emotion, and with unqualified assent.

" By what means, unless by the peculiar favour of God, did Arnaud escape falling into the hands of the Swiss catholics, who sought to lay hold of him, that he might suffer at Constance, like John Huss and Jerome of Prague? Is it not miraculous that a small band of men should force the bridge of Salabertran, guarded by 2500 men, kill 600 of them with the loss of fifteen only? Is it not as clear as the light of day, that it was by special permission that the Roman Catholics, who for three years had inhabited the houses of the Vaudois, should all fly on their approach, as well as the troops who ought to have defended them? Who but God could have inspired such a small party, without money and a thousand other requisites, courageously to undertake a war against the King of France, who then made all Europe tremble? And who but God could protect them, and cause them gloriously to succeed, in spite of every effort used by two mighty powers to exterminate them?

"Can any one be weak enough to suppose, that without Divine protection 367 Vaudois, shut up for eight months in La Balsille, sleeping on the earth, and subsisting only on bread and herbs, in small quantities, could force 10,000 French and 12,000 Piedmontese to retire with loss; and that after defending themselves for so long a time, they could have so happily escaped the fury of the French, who, still enraged at the obstinate resistance they met with from such a handful of men, had resolved to condemn them to be hung, and had actually brought executioners and ropes for that purpose?

"Weak as human nature is, every one must allow that the Almighty God fought for the Vaudois, assisting them whenever they were on the point of failing; and opening the eyes of their prince, and inducing him to seek their assistance against their joint enemy, after restoring them to their homes and own inheritance, as well as to their pure mode of worship. Does it not surpass imagination, that although these people were more than eighteen times engaged in battle during the efforts they made to penetrate into their valleys, they lost only thirty of their number; while their enemies lost altogether 10,000, men without effecting the object they had in view?

"After so many wonderful achievements, is it not clear that the arms of the enemy were blessed by the false benedictions of Rome, while theirs were strengthened by the protection of the great God, and King of Kings?"

CHAPTER XI.

THE fidelity and valour of the Vaudois to the Duke of Savoy, were of the utmost importance to that prince in his wars with France, in consequence of which new promises were made, and additional privileges conferred on these faithful people. But, alas! the ungrateful Victor Amadeus soon forgot both his promises and the obligations under which he lay to his Vaudois subjects. Immediately on the termination of the war with France, he issued an edict, "ordering all the Vaudois who were not natives of the valleys of Piedmont, to leave his dominions on pain of death." Such was the recompense which Victor Amadeus rendered to a people, whose loyalty and fidelity he had repeatedly acknowledged, and through whose instrumentality his very throne had been preserved.

Petitions and remonstrances were of no

avail. The ungrateful prince gave orders that his cruel edict should immediately be carried into effect; in consequence of which the greater part of the inhabitants who had been established in the valleys within forty years, together with those in the valley of Perosa, amounting altogether to the number of three thousand persons, were banished, in 1698, from the territories of the Duke of Savoy. To lessen their sufferings, he promised to furnish them with provisions till they were beyond the limits of the country from which they were expatriated; but no sooner had they begun their march, than this promise was also broken; and the poor exiles were left to procure for themselves a miserable subsistence. In this wretched condition they arrived at Geneva, with the intrepid Arnaud, who was among the number of the sufferers, where they were received with the greatest kindness. Scattered throughout the Protestant cantons of Switzerland, they were supported for some time by private charity, and by contributions which were raised for them in England and Holland. At length colonies of these exiles were established in the dominions of the Elector of Brandenburg, the Landgraves of Hesse Cassel, Darmstadt, and Homberg, &c.; and through the intercession of William, King of England, and of the Dutch government, provision was made for the greater part of them in the possessions of the duke of Wirtemberg. Of the ministers of the churches, seven, with their schoolmasters, were paid by the king of England who also, allowed M. Arnaud a pension to bring up his family; four ministers were paid by the States General, and the rest by their adopted sovereigns and their own churches. Thus kindly favoured by the princes, under whose mild laws they had taken shelter, they lived peaceably, praying God for the preservation of their benefactors, &c.

After the expulsion of the three thousand, liberty of conscience, not unmixed, however, with many vexations and trials, was enjoyed by the Vaudois who still inhabited the valleys of Piedmont. This was owing, under Divine Providence, to the powerful protection of the Protestant states of Europe, and in particular, to that of England. The pensions which had been granted by the English government to the Vaudois pastors from the national contributions which were made in 1665, were discontinued under the reigns of Charles II. and James II.; but in 1689, William and Mary renewed these pensions, which were not withdrawn by the English government till 1807, although no remittances were made to the poor Waldenses after 1797.

The difficulties with which the Waldenses have had to contend since their restoration by

Victor Amadeus, have been by no means of a trivial nature. Notwithstanding the numerous obligations under which that prince lay to these faithful people, he issued an edict, in 1721, "banishing the pastors and teachers from the valley of Pragela, forbidding the assembling of more than ten persons together in said valley for any purpose whatever, under the severest penalties." The interposition of foreign powers prevented, it is true, the former scenes of persecution from being renewed; but from time to time edicts of restriction were issued by the dukes of Savoy, which pressed so heavily on the afflicted Vaudois, that England was again called upon, in 1768, to send them pecuniary relief. The pensions which were given by William and Mary, "being found insufficient, in 1770, a general collection was made, the interest of which was paid under the name of the English National Subsidy. From these sums, the pastors received their incomes, amounting from 180 to 220 dollars, those of the most laborious parishes receiving the largest payment. The interest of the Dutch collections was applied to the salaries of the Dutch schoolmasters, widows of pastors, and retired pastors. And in Switzerland, studentships were established at the universities of Geneva, Lausanne, and Basle, for the young Vaudois intended for the ministry."

"In the year 1768, the king of England granted his royal letters patent in favour of the Protestants of the Vaudois churches in the valleys of Piedmont, to empower them to solicit the contributions of well disposed persons, 'to enable them to maintain the ministers, churches, schools, and poor, which they were not able to support in any tolerable manner.' The king also directed, that the amount of this charitable collection should be paid into the hands of the Incorporated Society for the Propagation of the Gospel in Foreign Parts, and be by them invested in government securities, the interest of which should be appropriated to the religious uses of the Protestant inhabitants of the valley of Piedmont. In obedience to these directions, the treasurer was empowered to receive the contributions, and carry into effect these designs; since which period, annual stipends have been regularly paid to the thirteen pastors of the valley of Piedmont, independently of certain small allowances to the widows of the deceased ministers. By the accumulation of the excess of interest, and other gratuities, the capital sum has been raised to £10,000, (44,444 dollars,) which has enabled the Society to extend the gross amount of the salaries to £292 (1298 dollars) per annum, for which sum the thirteen pastors draw upon the treasurer."

The affairs of the Waldenses remained in a state of comparative tranquillity till 1794. Previous to that period, it is true, they had been frequently exposed to many vexations, insults, and oppressions, from their Roman Catholic enemies, as well as to numerous hardships from the inhumanity of the dukes of Savoy: But it was not till the above-mentioned year that renewed efforts were made to destroy them. Ever anxious to show their enmity to Protestants, a horrible plot was then projected by the Papists to assassinate all the inhabitants of La Torre,—a plot which, contrary to all expectation, was most providentially frustrated by the activity of General Godin, a Swiss officer.

The season which the assassins chose for carrying their murderous purpose into execution, was when there were none in La Torre but aged men and helpless women and children. Every man capable of bearing arms was then engaged in the conflict between France and the allied army; but, while the Vaudois were thus honourably endeavouring to repel an invading foe, measures were devised for effecting their ruin. The 14th of May, at sun-set, was the time appointed for falling on the defenceless victims. M. Odetti, a captain of the Piedmontese militia, though a zealous Roman Catholic, was struck with horror at the base design, and on the very

day on which the work of slaughter was to
commence, he gave information of it to General Godin, who then commanded the Piedmontese troops on the nearest frontier. Giving
no credit to the intelligence of so foul a con-
spiracy, General Godin took no notice of the
repeated messages which were sent, communicating the dismal tidings. At length,
however, some of the wretched inhabitants
themselves arrived. The dreadful news flew
like lightning through the ranks of the Vaudois, and fathers and husbands were driven
almost to desperation. A few hours, only,
and the unhappy victims to Popish cruelty
would be no more. General Godin, therefore,
gave orders to march, when a scene the most
appalling was presented. Amidst the groan
of horror, and the scream of despair, the
frantic Vaudois flew, rather than marched,
to the relief of their families. Precipices
and torrents were utterly disregarded. They
flung themselves from one rock to another,
and plunged into rivers, dangers which nothing but desperation could have induced
them to encounter. To add to the afflicting
scene, the rain fell in torrents, the roads were
rendered almost impassable, and the very
heavens seemed to be set against their honourable purpose. Unmindful of the over-
whelming currents which poured from the
mountains, they dashed through the floods

which impeded their progress, and urged each other forward amidst shouts of despair, and the still more dreadful cries of distracted women who met them, and intimated that the work of slaughter was already commenced. At length they arrived within sight of La Torre, at the very moment when the bell tolled as the signal to shed the blood of the innocent. "We are too late," cried the wretched fathers and husbands, "but if we cannot prevent, we will revenge." The rush was tremendous: in a few seconds they were in the heart of La Torre, when numerous voices were heard from the inside of the barricaded houses, joyfully welcoming their intrepid deliverers.

The interposition of Divine Providence, throughout the whole of this affair, is most conspicuous. The few hours which intervened betwixt the time when the Vaudois received information of the intended massacre and the moment of its accomplishment;—the distance of the road which they had to travel;—the difficulties and dangers which they had to surmount ere they reached La Torre;—all seemed to render the attempt at saving the devoted victims utterly impracticable. What is impossible with men, is, however, easily accomplished by God. The very storm of rain, which to the Vaudois, at first, almost cut off the last ray of hope, proved the means of arresting the arm of the assassins. Terrified at the deluge, their murderous purpose was delayed till the moment the Vaudois appeared in La Torre, when the cowardly murderers fled, and escaped in the darkness of the night. To the honour of the Waldenses, they took no other revenge than that of forwarding a list of the names of the assassins to the government: But to the disgrace of the duke of Savoy, no notice whatever was taken of the matter; while general Godin, who had incurred the displeasure of the government by this act of kindness to the Vaudois, was shortly afterwards dismissed the service!

Thus, till the present time, have the Waldenses been persecuted for righteousness' sake,—a people " against whom," to use the words of Milner, when speaking of their forefathers, " malice could say no evil, but what admits the most satisfactory refutation: men distinguished for every virtue, and only hated because of godliness itself. Persecutors with a sigh owned, that, because of their virtue, they were the most dangerous enemies of the Church. But of what church ? Of that which, in the thirteenth century, and long before, had evidenced itself to be Antichristian. Here were not an individual or two, but very many real christians, who held the real doctrines of Scripture, and carefully

abstained from all the idolatry of the times.
How obdurate is the heart of man by nature!
Men could see and own the superior excel-
lence of these persons, and yet could barba-
rously persecute them! What a blessed light
is that of Scripture! By that the Waldenses saw the road to heaven, of which the
wisest of their contemporaries were ignorant,
who, though called christians, made no use
of the oracles of God."

Little alteration took place in the affairs of
the Vaudois till the year 1800, when Piedmont fell under the yoke of France. Previous to this period, it is true, a diminution
had taken place in the payments to the Vaudois pastors from Holland, and in 1797, those
from England were stopped altogether.* But
no sooner did Bonaparte become master of
the duke of Savoy's dominions, than, instead
of resenting the zeal which the Waldenses
had displayed against foreign invasion, he
ordered their pastors to be enrolled among
the clergy of the empire, assigned certain
sums from the treasury of Turin as an increase to their diminished stipends, which
raised their incomes to upwards of £60 (266

* As already mentioned, the English government
did not withdraw the pensions till 1807; but from some
mismanagement on the part of those to whom the
payments were entrusted, none were received by the
Vaudois after 1797.

dollars) per annum, and put the Vaudois in all respects upon an equal footing with the Roman catholics.

No sooner, however, was the house of Savoy restored to the throne, in 1814, than it refused to grant any privileges to the Waldenses beyond those which they enjoyed previous to the French revolution. The sums which were drawn from the treasury of Turin were stopped, and the families of several of the Vaudois ministers were for a time reduced to such necessity, that they were obliged to depend upon the charity of their neighbours for subsistence. It is true that both Charles Félix, the present sovereign of the Vaudois, and his predecessor Victor Emanuel, have treated their protestant subjects with much greater lenity than was ever experienced under former princes,—have always received the Waldensian deputies with kindness,—and have placed them under the same laws as their fellow subjects; yet none of them " can rise in the army above a sub-lieutenant; nor, in civil offices, beyond a notary, secretary, apothecary, or surgeon." The following are a few only of many grievances under which the Vaudois still labour: " No Protestant can inherit or purchase land beyond the limitations of the Clusone and Pelice: No books of instruction or devotion, for the use of the protestants, may be printed ın Piedmont:* No Vaudois may practice, as a physician, surgeon, apothecary, attorney, or advocate, except among his own community, and within the limits, &c. and although the protestant population in the valleys is, when compared with the catholic, as 1700 to 40, the catholics have the civil power.

" It frequently happens that a duly qualified Romanist cannot be found in the commune, to complete the number; and that the very refuse of the people have been nominated, to keep within the letter of the law. The protestants are obliged to observe the festivals of the papists, and to abstain from work on those days. This is another excessive hardship. There is one holiday, at least, every week, and sometimes two or three; so that the protesant peasant has seldom more than five days in the week for labour, and sometimes only three. The Sabbath day he keeps with scrupulous observance, while the Roman catholic cares not for violating it. A poor Vaudois peasant was accused of irrigating his little meadow on a festival day, and condemned to pay a fine, for not observing the sanctity of a saint's day. Fifteen cents a day in the winter, and twenty in the summer, is the utmost a peasant can earn: take away

* A very heavy duty, amounting almost to a prohibition, is laid upon works imported into the valleys.

two or three days from his weekly earnings, and what a pittance is left! Roasted chestnuts, potatoes, and bread, if any, of the blackest and most ordinary sort, is the principal food he can obtain."

With a philanthropy which does honour to himself, and may put to the blush many former travellers to that small but interesting portion of the protestant world, Mr. Gilly, who lately visited Piedmont, has advocated the claims of the poor and afflicted Vaudois in a manner which cannot fail to awaken the sympathy, and excite the generosity of the British nation. This effect has been already produced. Through his exertions and those of the Vaudois committee, the English government has renewed the royal grant, to give the former pensions to Waldensian pastors; and large sums have been collected otherwise, for the purpose of relieving the wants of that interesting people.

The present population of the three valleys amounts to nearly 19,000, about 1700 only of which are Roman Catholics. They are confined entirely within these three valleys, Lucerna, Perosa, and San Martino, and there exists an edict rendering them incapable of purchasing beyond these limits.

In regard to the character of the ancient Waldenses, their bitterest persecutors were forced to bear testimony to the uprightnes, integrity, and purity of life, of these witnesses for the truth. " These heretics," says an inquisitor who wrote against them, "are known by their manners and conversation, for they are orderly and modest in their behaviour and deportment. They avoid all appearance of pride in their dress; they neither indulge in finery of attire, nor are they remarkable for being mean or ragged. They get their livelihood by manual industry, as day-labourers or mechanics. and their teachers are weavers or tailors. They are not anxious about amassing riches, but content themselves with the necessaries of life. They are chaste, temperate, and sober, and abstain from anger. Even when they work, they either learn or teach. In like manner, also, their women are very modest, avoiding backbiting, foolish jesting, and levity of speech, especially abstaining from lies or swearing."—" Their heresy excepted," says Claudius Seisselius, Archbishop of Turin, " they generally live a purer life than any other Christians. They are perfectly irreprehensible, and without reproach among men, addicting themselves to the service of God with all their might." Yet this prelate not only wrote against, but joined in persecuting them, simply because they would not submit to all the absurdities of the Popish Church!

Thuanus the historian, a Roman Catholic,

thus describes the inhabitants of the valley of
Fraissiniere in Dauphiny:—"Their clothing,"
says he, " is of the skins of sheep—they have
no linen. They inhabit seven villages; their
houses are constructed of flint stone, with a
flat roof, covered with mud, which when
spoiled or loosened by rain, they smooth again
with a roller. In these they live with their
cattle, separated from them, however, by a
fence; they have, besides, two caves, set
apart for particular purposes, in one of which
they conceal their cattle, in the other themselves, when hunted by their enemies. They
live on milk and venison, being by constant
practice excellent marksmen. Poor as they
are, they are content, and live separate from
the rest of mankind. One thing is very remarkable, that persons externally rude, should
have so much moral cultivation. They can
read and write. They know French sufficient
for the understanding of the Bible and the
singing of Psalms. You can scarcely find a
boy who cannot give an intelligent account
of the faith they profess. In this indeed *they
resemble their brethren of the other valleys.*
They pay tribute with a good conscience, and
the obligation of this duty is peculiarly noted
in the confessions of their faith. If, by reason of the civil wars, they are prevented from
doing this, they carefully set apart the sum,

and at the first opportunity pay it to the king's tax gatherers."

During the time of the great persecutions of the inhabitants of Merindol and Provence, in 1540, the Bishop of Cavaillon sent a monk to hold a conference with them, in order to convince them of their errors, and that thus the further effusion of blood might be prevented. But the monk soon returned in confusion, acknowledging that in his whole life he had never known so much of the Scriptures as he had learned during the few days he had been conversing with those heretics. The Bishop, however, sent a number of doctors, young men, who had lately come from the Sorbonne, at Paris. But one of them on his return confessed, that he had understood more of the doctrine of salvation from the answers of the children in their catechisms, than by all the disputations that he had ever before heard.

Two ecclesiastics, deputed by Francis I. to visit the Waldenses of Provence, returned with the following account of the *heretics*, as they were termed, to that monarch:—"They are a laborious race of people, who, about two hundred years ago, emigrated from Piedmont, to dwell in Provence. Betaking themselves to husbandry and feeding of cattle, they have restored many villages destroyed by the wars,

and rendered other desert and uncultivated
places extremely fertile by their industry.
By the information given us in the country
of Provence, we find them to be a very peaceable people, beloved by their neighbours, men
of good behaviour, of godly conversation,
faithful to their promises, and punctual in
paying their debts. They are a charitable
people, not permitting any among them to fall
into want. They are, moreover, liberal to
strangers, and the travelling poor, as far as
their ability extends. And the inhabitants
of Provence affirm, that they are a people
who cannot endure to blaspheme, or name the
devil, or swear at all, unless in making some
solemn contracts, or in judgment. Finally,
they are well known by this, that if they happen to be cast into any company where the
conversation is loose or blasphemous, to the
dishonour of God, they instantly withdraw."

Importuned by the calumnies of informers,
Louis XII. of France also sent two respect-
able persons into Provence to make inquiry,
and return him a faithful account of the Waldenses. They accordingly reported, "That
in visiting all their parishes and places of worship, they found no images, nor signs of the
ornaments belonging to the mass, nor any
Romish ceremonies; but that they could not
discover any marks of the crimes with which

they were charged. On the contrary, the
Sabbath was strictly observed, and their chil‐
dren instructed in the articles of the Chris‐
tian faith, and the commandments of God."
Having heardthe report, Louis declared with
an oath, "They are better men than myself
or my people."

Such are the testimonies of a few of the
enemies and persecutors of the Vaudois, to
the strict purity, and unimpeachable integ‐
rity of their lives. To these we might add,
were it necessary, those of the Reformers,
and of many eminent Protestant historians.
Enough, however, has been stated relative to
the ancient Vaudois; and we shall now con‐
clude this short account of these faithful fol
lowers of the Lamb, by giving a few testimo‐
nies to the character of the present inhabitants
of Piedmont, collected from the works of
modern writers.

"Among the most striking instances of the
piety and virtue of the Waldenses of the pre‐
sent time," says Mr. Acland, "is the absence
of drunkenness, swearing, sensual profligacy,
and that inordinate love of gain, to the sacri‐
fice of all honour and honesty, too frequently
met with in the neighbouring population.
They are also distinguished by a more re‐
spectful demeanour to their superiors, more
attention to cleanliness, and less to gaudy

show, more industry, and, singularly enough, more loyalty to their sovereign."

"The Vaudois," says Mr. Sims, "preserve from their forefathers a sincere respect for pure and undefiled religion. They are remarkably honest, hospitable, and humane; and even give what they can spare to the destitute of other communities."

"And," says Mr. Jackson, "I have no hesitation in saying, that I think the Vaudois, even in their present circumstances, the most moral people in Europe. During my residence in the valleys of Piedmont, I never saw an instance of drunkenness, nor was offended by hearing a single oath of swearing or blasphemy."

"Much as I was prejudiced in favour of this extraordinary race," says Mr. Gilly, "before I became personally acquainted with their character, that acquaintance has increased my admiration of them. If innocence, and pure religion, can be said to reign any where, it is here; and all my inquiries and researches have had the effect of bringing the firm conviction to my mind, that they are one of those favoured people whom the arm of the Almighty has providentially shielded, for purposes best known to his inscrutable wisdom. Their morals correspond with their faith; and their lives and conversations testify, that the doctrines they profess are

those of the truth; for nothing short of a firm
persuasion that they are burning and shining
lights, which are not to be put out, could
have given them courage and perseverance
sufficient to withstand the temptations to
which their spiritual integrity has been exposed, or to resist the strong hand which has
been lifted up against them for more than ten
centuries."

APPENDIX.

Chronological Table of a few eminent persons and remarkable events in the History of the Waldenses.

A. D.

The title of Cathari, or, The Pure, corresponding with the English term Puritan, it would appear, was first given to the followers of Novation, a Romish pastor, who resisted the Papal corruptions, - - - - - 251

Sylvester, Bishop of Rome, whose haughty conduct is said to have been the cause of the first protest of the churches of the valleys, - . - - 314

Ambrose, Bishop of Milan, protests against the Romish superstitions, - 374

Nine bishops rejected the communion of the Pope as heretical in 553, or 590

Paulinas, Bishop of Aquileia, condemns the decrees of the second Council of Nice, - - - - - 787

Claude, Bishop of Turin, and of the valleys of Piedmont, combats the idolatries of Rome, - - - - 817

The Paterines were numerous at Milan in 1026, and - - - - 1040

A. D.

The Noble Lesson, written by a Waldensian pastor, - - - - 1100

A Treatise against Antichrist, written by another Waldensian pastor, 1120

Evervinus writes to St. Bernard against the Waldenses, - - 1140

Some of the Cathari are persecuted in England, - - - - - 1159

Peter Waldo attaches himself to the Waldenses, - - - - 1160

Pope Lucius III. publishes an edict against them, - - - - 1181'

Another edict, published against them by Ildefonsus, King of Arragon, - 1194

Inquisition established for the suppression of the Waldenses, - - 1204

Council of Lateran against heretics, 1215

Bull of Pope John XXII. against the Waldenses, - - - - 1332

Suppression of the Waldensian churches in France from 1230 to - 1350

Walter Lollard, a Vaudois pastor, burnt at Cologne, - - - 1350

Bull of Pope Clement VII. against the Vaudois, - - - - 1370

The first severe persecution against the Waldenses in the valleys of Pragela and Perosa, - - - - - 1400

Bull of Innocent VIII. against the inhabitants of the valleys, - - 1487

Articles of Faith drawn up and pre-

A. D.

March of the exiles under Henri Arnaud to recover Piedmont - - 1689

Their restoration to their native valleys, - - - - - - 1690

Three thousand of the Waldenses banished, - - - - - 1698

Edict of Victor Amadeus II. against the Vaudois, - - - - 1730

A general collection throughout England in their behalf, - - - 1768

The pension from England discontinued, - - - - - - 1797

Piedmont falls under the yoke of France, - - - - - 1800

The King of Sardinia restored to his throne, and annuls the laws in favour of the Waldenses which had been granted by Napoleon, - - - 1814

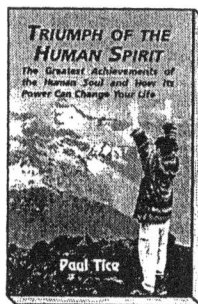

www.ingramcontent.com/pod-product-compliance
Lightning Source LLC
Chambersburg PA
CBHW031845090426
42741CB00005B/354